Enduring Freedom

Anders Lustgarten

finboroughtheatre
Giant Steps

First published in 2008 by Giant Steps Limited,
41 Parfrey Street, London, W6 9EW.

Printed by Polprint – 63 Jeddo Road, London W12 9EE, UK.
Tel.+44-(0)20-8749-0777, e-mail polprint@talktalk.net

A CIP record for this book is available from the British Library.

ISBN: 978-0-9560201-0-9

Cover design: Rebecca Maltby.

Cover image: Vanessa Hawkins

finboroughtheatre

Giant Steps

Enduring Freedom
by Anders Lustgarten

World premiere at the Finborough Theatre
as part of the [**finborough**playwrights season]:
Wednesday, 6 August 2008

Enduring Freedom

by Anders Lustgarten

Cast in order of appearance
Susan McFarlane **Lisa Eichhorn**
Tom McFarlane **Vincent Riotta**
Hanna Schneider **Fiz Marcus**
Ray Villapiano **Charlie Roe**
Sophia Villapiano **Anna Savva**
Linda Brown **Anna Savva**
Park Attendant **Charlie Roe**
The Mad Dog **Charlie Roe**
Diane Roberts **Fiz Marcus**
Jessica Taylor **Anna Savva**

The action largely takes place in New Jersey from Autumn 2001 to Autumn 2003.

The performance lasts approximately ninety minutes.

There will be one interval of fifteen minutes.

Our patrons are respectfully reminded that, in this intimate theatre, any noise such as rustling programmes, talking or the ringing of mobile phones may distract the actors and your fellow audience-members.

Directed by **Roland Jaquarello**
Designed by **Vanessa Hawkins**
Lighting by **Gabriel Phillips-Sanchez**
Sound by **David Sharrock**
Assistant Direction by **Georgina Guy**
Assistant Designer **Kimberley Turner**
Assistant Lighting Designer / Technical Operator **Martin Ellsmore**
Graphic Design **Rebecca Maltby**
Production Photography **Robert Workman**
Presented by **Giant Steps Limited** in association with **Neil McPherson** for the **Finborough Theatre**

Lisa Eichhorn Susan McFarlane
Trained at RADA.
Theatre includes *Hamlet, As You Like It, Much Ado About Nothing, The Fatal Weakness, Arms and the Man, Tonight at 8.30, The Novelist,* and *Golden Boy* (National Theatre), *Winding the Ball, Misfits, Tobaccoland* and *Six Degrees of Separation* (Royal Exchange Theatre, Manchester), *The Women of Lockerbie* (Orange Tree Theatre, Richmond), and *Shadowlands* (Salisbury Playhouse).
In New York City, she has appeared on Broadway in *The Speed of Darkness* (Belasco Theater), and *Any Given Day* (Longacre Theater), and Off Broadway in *The Common Pursuit* (Promenade Theater), *The Summer Winds* (Naked Angels), *Down the Road* (Atlantic Theater), and *Betrayal* (The Actors Studio).
Television and Film includes *The Weather in the Streets, Cutter's Way* (Best Actress Award at Deauville), *The Europeans* (BAFTA nomination), *Yanks* (2 Golden Globe nominations), *East Lynne, The Wall, Inspector Morse, Midsomer Murders, Spooks, Jericho, Cracker, Law and Order, Murder in Three Acts,* and *The Practice.*

Fiz Marcus Hanna Schneider / Diane Roberts
Trained at Bristol University.
At the Finborough Theatre, Fiz has appeared in *Little Squares* and *A Man with Connections.*
Other Theatre includes *Equus* (National Tour), *On Saturdays this Bed is Poland* (New Perspectives National Tour), *My Matisse* (Jermyn Street Theatre), *Private Lives* (Haymarket Theatre, Basingstoke), *Red Princess* (Red Shift), *A Man with Connections* (Minerva Theatre, Chichester, Finborough Theatre and The Arches, Glasgow), *Four Portraits - of Mothers* (Bridewell Theatre), *Lovers and Lies* (National Tour, the Czech Republic and the Netherlands), *Release* (Tristan Bates Theatre), *The Hidden Winter* (Soho Theatre), *A Kind of Alaska* (Orange Tree Theatre, Richmond), *Lorenzaccio* (Young Vic), *Star Quality* (Apollo Theatre and National Tour), *The Wedding* (National Theatre Studio), *A Small Family Business* and *The Stronger* (Chichester Festival Theatre), *Haven* (Bridewell Theatre), *The Homecoming* (Comedy Theatre), *Small Objects of Desire* (Soho Theatre), *Daisy Pulls It Off* (Leatherhead Theatre), and *Happy Family* (Redgrave Theatre, Farnham).
Television includes *Jekyll, The Amazing Mrs Pritchard, Mayo, Wild West, Life and Death, The Bill,* and *The Sharp End.*
Film includes *Swinging with the Finkels, A Bout De Truffe, The Penalty King, Oxford Park, Out of Breath, Suzie Gold,* and *Leon the Pig Farmer.*

Vincent Riotta Tom McFarlane
Trained at RADA.
Theatre includes *Romeo and Juliet, A View from the Bridge* and *Flashpoint* (Young Vic), *The Corsican Brothers* (Abbey Theatre, Dublin), *A Streetcar Named Desire* and *All My Sons* (Haymarket Theatre, Leicester), and *Fridays at Seven* (Court Theatre, West Hollywood).
Television includes *Coronation Street, The Bill, A Touch of Frost, Monk, Alias, JAG, Capo Dei Capi* and *Falcone.*
Film includes *Captain Corelli's Mandolin, Heaven, Under the Tuscan Sun,* and *A Little Worm* (Best Actor Award at the Barcelona Film Festival).
He also directed the feature film *Deadly Weapon,* starring John Savage.

Charlie Roe Ray Villapiano / The Mad Dog / Park Attendant
Theatre includes *To Kill a Mockingbird* (West Yorkshire Playhouse and National Tour), *A Few Good Men* (Theatre Royal, Haymarket), *The Day After the Fair* (Lyric Theatre), *Electra* (Gate Theatre), *The Taming of the Shrew* and *Rosencrantz and Guildenstern are Dead* (English Touring Theatre), *Philoctetes* and *The Tempest* (Cheek by Jowl), *Macbeth* and *Waiting for Godot* (Lyric Theatre, Belfast), *As You Like It, Six Characters in Search of an Author* and *Ting Tang Mine* (National Theatre), *The Lady's Not for Burning* (Chichester Festival Theatre), *Troilus and Cressida* (Royal Shakespeare Company), and *A Month in the Country* (Leatherhead Theatre).
Television includes *Derailed, If, Wire in the Blood, The Lakes, Peak Practice, Kavanagh QC, Silent Witness, Inspector Morse, Minder, Shackleton,* and *Brideshead Revisited*.

Anna Savva Sophia Villapiano / Linda Brown / Jessica Taylor
Trained at LAMDA.
Theatre includes *Frida and Diego* (Red Shift – nominated for *Time Out* Award for Best Actress), *Kvetch* (West Yorkshire Playhouse), *Four Horsemen of the Apocalypse* and *Salome* (Citizens' Theatre, Glasgow), *Carmen* (Derby Playhouse), *A View from the Bridge* (Liverpool Playhouse), *A Midsummer Night's Dream* (Royal Exchange Theatre, Manchester), *Snow Queen* (Theatr Clwyd), *Blood Wedding* (Haymarket Theatre, Leicester), *Hiawatha* (Crucible Theatre, Sheffield), *Macbeth* (Cherub Theatre), *Hot Fudge and Ice Cream* (Contact Theatre, Manchester), *Beauty and the Beast* (Library Theatre, Manchester), *Prometheus Bound*, performed in Greek, and *Alcestes* (Theatro Technis), *Peter Pan* (ICA), *Measure for Measure* (Arcola Theatre), and *The Battle of Green Lanes* (Theatre Royal, Stratford East).
Film includes *Restoration, The Quiet Assassin, Grandma's Funeral,* and *Taxi*.
Television includes *EastEnders, Sharpe's Honour, London's Burning, The Chief, Yo Picasso, Minder, Family,* and *Planespotting*.
Radio includes *Orient Express, Assassins, Hamam Bride, Queen of the Potatoes, Captain Corelli's Mandolin, Crown of Wild Myrtle, The Silk Worm,* and *A Matter of Sex*.

Anders Lustgarten Playwright
At the Finborough Theatre, Anders' first play *The Insurgents*, a comic drama about Kurdish immigration and political resistance to globalisation, was produced as part of a double bill *A Letter to England* in 2007, while *Enduring Freedom* received workshops through the Finborough Theatre's Literary Department in both March 2007 and April 2008. Anders is currently also under commission at the Soho Theatre, for whom he is writing a play about black prisoners and Islam and a musical about the BNP. A British writer of American parentage, Anders works as a political activist as well as a playwright, specialising in putting pressure on the corporations, governments and banks backing the world's most egregious 'development' projects. He is shortly to begin devising a play in and about Zimbabwe for a tour around southern Africa later this year.

Roland Jaquarello Director
Roland has been a Resident Director at the Abbey Theatre Dublin and Artistic Director of the Lyric Theatre Belfast, the Redgrave Theatre Farnham, Live Theatre Newcastle, and his own company Green Fields and Far Away which toured Irish work in the UK. He was also Assistant Director to Lindsay Anderson on David Storey's *The Contractor* at the Royal Court Theatre and Senior Producer with Radio Drama BBC Northern Ireland.
His many productions include *After The Fall, All My Sons, The Iceman Cometh, Cat on a Hot Tin Roof* and *Mrs Warren's Profession* (Lyric Theatre, Belfast), *The School for Scandal , Escurial, Fando and Lis*

and *Picnic on the Battlefield* (Abbey Theatre, Dublin), *Miss Julie, The Exception and the Rule* and *The Car Cemetery* (Welsh Drama Company), *A Touch of the Poet* and *The Shadow of a Gunman* (Green Fields), *George Dandin* and *The Playboy of the Western World* (Redgrave Theatre, Farnham), Slawomir Mrozek's *Police*, Joe Orton's *Loot* and *What The Butler Saw* (all Dublin), *It's a Two Foot Six Inches Above the Ground World* (National Tour), *Androcles and the Lion* (Everyman Theatre, Liverpool), and *An Inspector Calls* (Peterborough Theatre).

During the 1980s, with Tim Woodward, he produced a series of European and American plays in London at fringe theatres of which he directed Pirandello's *Naked* and *The Man with the Flower in his Mouth*, Ernst Toller's *Hinkemann* and Howard Fast's *30 Pieces of Silver*. He has also directed many new plays including *Hatchet* by Heno Magee (Abbey Theatre, Dublin and Half Moon Theatre, London), *King Herod Advises* by Conor Cruise O'Brien (Abbey Theatre, Dublin), *The Ikon Maker* by Desmond Hogan (Green Fields Tour and Gate Theatre, London), *Jack Doyle – The Man who Boxed Like John McCormick!* by Ian McPherson (Green Fields and Lyric Theatre, Hammersmith), *A Flag Unfurled* by Leigh Jackson (Green Fields), *The Death of Humpty Dumpty* by Graham Reid (Live Theatre, Newcastle), *Culture Vultures* by Robin Glendinning, *The Butterfly of Killybegs* by Brian Foster (Lyric Theatre, Belfast), and *A New York State of Mind* by Sam McCready (Opera House, Belfast).

His work in broadcasting includes work by Brian Friel, Sebastian Barry and John Arden for Radio 3. For Radio 4, his many productions include work by Colm McCann, Gary Mitchell, Kaite O'Reilly, John Arden, Larry Gelbart, Mark Lawson and J.M. Synge. His production of William Trevor's *The Property of Colette Nervi* was nominated for the Prix Italia Play Section in 1990, and Martin Lynch's modern Belfast version of *An Enemy of the People*, for Radio 3, recently won an O.Z. Whitehead Award from the Irish Playwrights and Screenwriters Guild for Best Radio Script 2007. He has also produced documentaries on Van Morrison, Joni Mitchell, Mel Torme and Marlon Brando for Radio 2.

Vanessa Hawkins Designer

Vanessa started her career working in the design departments of Watford Palace Theatre and the National Theatre. She was Assistant Designer for The English Theatre of Hamburg and worked for several years at the Redgrave Theatre, Farnham, where she was Costume Designer for *The Jungle Book*.

Designs for theatre include *Enemy, Adam Redundant* and *Shakers Restirred* (London Repertory Company), *The Sea, The Accrington Pals* and *The Madwoman of Chaillot*, (Central School of Speech and Drama), *Skid 180* (Contact Theatre, Manchester, and Sydney Opera House) and *The Meeting Place* (The Green Room, Manchester). She was nominated for Best Set Design in *The Irish Times* Theatre Awards for *The Butterfly of Killybegs*, also directed by Roland Jaquarello (Lyric Theatre, Belfast).

Television includes Art Director on over twenty television drama episodes including *Hollyoaks*.

Film includes Art Director on the short film *Weaver's Wife*, directed by David Yates, and Designer for *BRO9* which won an award for Best Short Film at the BFI London and also for *A Pint in Purgatory* which won Best International Short in the New York Film Festival 2008. She recently designed her first feature film *The Crew*, due for release later this year.

Gabriel Phillips-Sanchez Lighting

Trained on the Lighting Design and Stage Electrics course at RADA.

Lighting Designs include *Jekyll and Hyde* (React Theatre), *Ursula* (RADA), *Shot Actress* (Full Story), *Simply the Best* (Pineapple Performing Arts at the Unicorn Theatre), and *Debbie Curtis Big Band* (Her Majesty's Theatre).

David Sharrock Sound

Trained in Theatre Sound Design at The Central School of Speech and Drama. He is a Sound Designer, Production Engineer, composer and musician. Sound Designs include *On the Avenue* and *Night at the Movies* (Northampton). Operation and crew roles include *Sfumanto* (Victoria and Albert Museum, part of the *Collaborators* exhibit), *My Life with the Dogs* and *Late Music* (BAC), *Two* (Courtyard Studio Theatre), and *Chicago* (Cambridge Theatre).

Georgina Guy Assistant Director

Studied at Oxford University, RADA and King's College London. She was awarded Best Director at the Oxford University New Writing Festival 2006 for her production of the Cameron Mackintosh Award winning script *BANK*. She is Artistic Director of Grey Light Productions and has directed for the company productions including *BANK and Other Plays* (King's Head Theatre), *Uncle Barry* (Blue Elephant Theatre) and *American Voices* (Greenwich Playhouse). As Assistant Director, she has assisted Brigid Panet on *The Tempest* (RADA). During 2007, Georgina worked as a Student Representative for the Donmar Warehouse and as an intern in the Literary Department at the Royal Court Theatre.

Giant Steps

Giant Steps has been founded by Roland Jaquarello to present a variety of new and challenging work. More information online at www.rolandjaquarello.com

finboroughtheatre
www.finboroughtheatre.co.uk

Artistic Director – Neil McPherson
Associate Director – Kate Wasserberg
Resident Designer – Alex Marker
Playwrights-in-Residence – James Graham, Peter Oswald, Al Smith, Laura Wade, Alexandra Wood
Literary Manager – Jane Fallowfield
General Manager – Rosie Jackson
Company Manager – Rachel Payant
Development Producer – Rachael Williams
The Finborough Theatre is grateful for the support of The Invicta Trust

Friends of the **finborough***theatre*

The Finborough Theatre receives no public funding, and relies solely on the support of our audiences. Please do consider supporting us by becoming a member of our Friends Scheme. There are four categories of Friends, each offering a wide range of benefits.

Brandon Thomas Friends – Anonymous. Nancy Balaban. Philip Beckley. Philip Hooker. David Humphrys. Barbara Marker. Harry MacAuslan. Maurice Lewendon. Anthony Melnikoff. Barbara Naughton. Sylvia Young.

Richard Tauber Friends – Charles Lascelles.

Lionel Monckton Friends – Anonymous.

William Terriss Friends – Leo Liebster.

Smoking is not permitted in the auditorium and the use of cameras and recording equipment is strictly prohibited.

In accordance with the requirements of the Royal Borough of Kensington and Chelsea: 1. The public may leave at the end of the performance by all doors and such doors must at that time be kept open. 2. All gangways, corridors, staircases and external passageways intended for exit shall be left entirely free from obstruction whether permanent or temporary. 3. Persons shall not be permitted to stand or sit in any of the gangways intercepting the seating or to sit in any of the other gangways.

The Finborough Theatre is licensed by the Royal Borough of Kensington and Chelsea to The Steam Industry. The Steam Industry is under the Artistic Direction of Phil Willmott. www.philwillmott.co.uk The Steam Industry is a company limited by guarantee. Registered in England no. 3448268. Registered Charity no. 1071304. Registered Office: 118 Finborough Road, London SW10 9ED.

For Giant Steps Limited

Directors – Roland Jaquarello and Mira Faber

Giant Steps is a company limited by guarantee. Registered in England and Wales no. 6553582. Registered Office: 41 Parfrey Street, London, W6 9EW.

finboroughtheatre

The multi-award-winning Finborough Theatre led by Artistic Director Neil McPherson presents new writing from the UK and overseas, Music Theatre and rediscoveries of forgotten work from the 19th and 20th centuries.

Founded in 1980, artists working at the theatre in its first decade included Rory Bremner, Clive Barker, Kathy Burke, Nica Burns, Ken Campbell and Clare Dowie. In the early 1990s, the theatre was at the forefront of new writing with Naomi Wallace's first play *The War Boys*; Rachel Weisz in David Farr's *Neville Southall's Washbag* which later became the award-winning West End play, *Elton John's Glasses*; and three plays by Anthony Neilson - *The Year of the Family, Normal* and *Penetrator*, which went on to play at the Royal Court. From 1994, the theatre was run by The Steam Industry. Highlights included new plays by Tony Marchant, David Eldridge, Mark Ravenhill and Phil Willmott, new writing development including Mark Ravenhill's *Shopping and F***king* (Royal Court, West End and Broadway) and Naomi Wallace's *Slaughter City* (Royal Shakespeare Company), the UK premiere of David Mamet's *The Woods*, and Anthony Neilson's *The Censor*, which transferred to the Royal Court.

Since 2000, New British plays have included Laura Wade's London debut with her adaptation of W.H. Davies' *Young Emma*, and James Graham's *Eden's Empire* (both commissioned specially for the Finborough Theatre); Simon Vinnicombe's *Year 10* which went on to play at BAC's *Time Out* Critics' Choice Season; James Graham's *Albert's Boy* with Victor Spinetti; Joy Wilkinson's *Fair* which transferred to the West End, Nicholas de Jongh's *Plague Over England* with Jasper Britton, David Burt and Nichola McAuliffe; and Stewart Permutt's *Many Roads to Paradise* with Miriam Karlin. London premieres have included Sonja Linden's *I Have Before Me a Remarkable Document Given to Me by a Young Lady from Rwanda*; and Jack Thorne's *Fanny and Faggot* which also transferred to the West End.

UK premieres of foreign plays have included Brad Fraser's *Wolfboy*; Lanford Wilson's *Sympathetic Magic*; Larry Kramer's *The Destiny of Me*; Tennessee Williams' *Something Cloudy; Something Clear*; Frank McGuinness' *Gates of Gold* with William Gaunt and the late John Bennett in his last stage role (which also transferred to the West End); *Hortensia and the Museum of Dreams* with Linda Bassett; *Blackwater Angel* – the UK debut of Irish playwright Jim Nolan – with Sean Campion; Joshua Sobol's *IWitness*; and the English premiere of Robert McLellan's Scots language classic, *Jamie the Saxt*.

Rediscoveries of neglected work have included the first London revivals of Rolf Hochhuth's *Soldiers*, and *The Representative*; both parts of Keith Dewhurst's *Lark Rise to Candleford* – performed in promenade and in repertoire; *The Women's War* – an evening of original suffragette plays; the Victorian comedy *Masks and Faces*; *Etta Jenks* with Clarke Peters and Daniela Nardini; *The Gigli Concert* with Niall Buggy and Paul McGann; *Loyalties* by John Galsworthy; Noël Coward's first play, *The Rat Trap*; T.W. Robertson's *Ours*; and Charles Wood's *Jingo* with Susannah Harker.

Music Theatre has included the new (premieres from the UK and USA by Grant Olding, Charles Miller, Michael John LaChuisa, Adam Guettel and Andrew Lippa) and the old (the sell-out Celebrating British Music Theatre series reviving forgotten British musicals).

The Finborough Theatre was the only unfunded theatre to be awarded the prestigious Pearson Playwriting Award bursary for Chris Lee in 2000, Laura Wade in 2005, James Graham in 2006 and Al Smith in 2007 – as well as the Pearson Award for Best Play for Laura Wade in 2005 and James Graham in 2007. The Finborough Theatre also won the Empty Space Peter Brook Mark Marvin Award in 2004, and was the inaugural winner of the Empty Space Peter Brook Award's Dan Crawford Pub Theatre Award in 2005.

You can read more about at the theatre at **www.finboroughtheatre.co.uk**

Enduring Freedom

Anders Lustgarten

This play is dedicated to the robbed, 2000-2008

Characters in order of appearance

Susan McFarlane, early fifties
Tom McFarlane, mid fifties
Hanna Schneider, mid forties
Ray Villapiano, mid fifties
Sophia Villapiano, late forties
Linda Brown, early forties
Park Attendant, male, fifties
The Mad Dog, male, early fifties but claims to be mid forties
Diane Roberts, mid forties
Jessica Taylor, early forties

This play requires five actors.
The characters of Hanna and Diane are doubled.
The characters of Ray, Park Attendant and The Mad Dog are doubled.
The characters of Sophia, Linda and Jessica are doubled.

The playwright would like to thank Laurence Lustgarten, Donna Dickenson, Annabel Capper, Esther Baker, Zena Birch, Stephanie Street, Roland Jaquarello, Mira Faber, Ben Hall, Lily Williams, Nina Steiger, Rebecca Lenkiewicz, Simon Stephens, Nick Hildyard, Sarah Harrington, Jack Hemens, Anna Schmidt and the Finborough Theatre including Kate Wasserberg and everyone who took part in the workshops.

Enduring Freedom

Spotlight on a large wooden cart with rubber wheels and rows of parallel handles sticking off a pole protruding from the front. In the cart stands an enormous granite tombstone, six feet high, two thousand pounds in weight. On the tombstone are carved the words "Unknown Civilians Killed in War." The flags of the United States and the United Nations flutter from the back of the cart.

Spotlight down. Cart is backlit so the stone looms ominously over the action, serving as Twin Tower, gravestone, monolith. Blackout.

Act One

Scene One

Lights up on the McFarlane home, Paterson, New Jersey, two days after September 11 2001. Night. On the table, along with bunches of flowers and other gifts, there are three places set for dinner. TV is on but with the sound off, flickering with endless talking heads and pictures of the attack.

Tom in the doorway. Susan at the table. Pause.

Susan: Nothing?

Tom: Nothing. (*Beat*) You?

Susan: Nothing.

They run together and cling on tightly. The TV flickers over their heads. Long pause.

Tom: (*indicating TV*) Can we please turn that off?

Susan: Sure. (*She turns it off with the remote*) I just—

Tom: I know.

Susan: I can't watch…and yet I can't not, you know?

Tom: I been the same.

Susan: The only thing you can do to help is watch. (*Beat*) I've been cleaning all day.

Tom: You hate cleaning.

Susan: I know that.

Tom: (*picking up a couple of teacups*) I didn't even know we still had these.

Susan: Well we do. And they're *clean*.

Tom: Come sit with me.

Susan: Just...gimme a couple more minutes.

Tom: Susie...

Susan: A couple more minutes. (*She picks up a cup. He takes it from her and puts it down*) But what if it's this one it depends on? I clean this one, he's OK, I don't...? What if it's this one keeping him alive? What if it's this glass, that plate...?

Beat.

Tom: I wouldn't walk on any cracks today. Took me twenty minutes to get the guys' coffees.

Susan: They should be getting coffee for you.

Tom: Nah, I offered. Something to do.

Beat.

Susan: The imagination is an extraordinary thing, isn't it?

Tom kisses Susan strongly. She responds. They stop kissing, but still hold each other tight for a while. They break. Beat.

Lot of people here today.

Tom: Yeah? Who?

Susan: My whole class, for one. More kids than ever actually *come* to class. I guess that boosted my attendance rate so it's an ill wind, huh? (*Pained smile. Beat*) All hiding behind each other and peering into the house. Kids can't believe their teacher lives like other people, can they?

Tom: I thought my teacher lived upside down in a cave and came out at night to drink blood.

Susan: And then Vinnie Palantonio, for whom "Go Jets" is a major feat of oratory, steps forward and looks me right in the eye and says, "We hope he comes home soon," and hands me this huge bunch of flowers. And then they all turn around as one, without another word, and they go back to school.

Beat.

Tom: Good. That's good.

Susan: Mrs Thompson was here.

Tom: Jeanie Thompson?

Susan: (*laughing*) Bush's best buddy, the very same.

Tom: Thought she pledged never to talk to you again after you voted Gore?

Susan: Brought that fruit basket over there.

Tom: You're kidding me.

Susan: They treating you OK over there, baby?

Tom: Yeah. Yeah. It's OK. It's fine. (*Beat*) There's nothing to do, Susie. *Nothing.* Nobody calls in. Like even fires are too scared to break out. And we can't get down there, not a chance, because who the fuck are we, just some bridge and tunnel Jersey crew *way* down the pecking order…

Susan: I guess everybody wants to help.

Tom: They can't think what to say to me, the guys. They tiptoe around me like I'm a bomb's gonna go off. I laughed out loud today, something in the funny paper, and they looked across all shocked and shit, like I swore in church. Made me feel like I done something wrong. Even Ray, you know? God bless him, all day long with the "We're gonna get them, Tommy. We're gonna pay these motherfuckers back. We're gonna get them."

Susan: Good old Ray.

Tom: Giving me the clenched fist across the room. The stuff you've always hated him doing, basically.

Susan: Right now I'd actually kinda like to see him—

Tom: And it ain't like I don't wanna pound somebody, anybody, you know?

Susan: Oh, I know.

Tom: But…I don't know. That ain't it. In the end I had to say to him, "Ray, much as I appreciate your support here, what I really wanna 'get' right now is my son." And he looks at me like—

Susan: We are lucky to have such good friends.

Tom: That is true. (*Beat. Straightforwardly*) There's a couple of things I don't understand, Susie. About what happened. About the pl—

Susan: I made lasagne.

Beat.

Tom: I ain't hungry.

Susan: Sure?

Tom: Real sure.

Susan: Me either. Wasn't hungry when I started, wasn't hungry when I finished. So I made another one. What kind of thinking is that?

They smile fragilely. She comes to him suddenly.

Susan: Where is he?

Where is he, Tom? Where is he? Where is he?

Tom: It's OK.

Susan: But where?

Tom: He's here, he's coming, he'll be here, it's OK.

Susan: I'm so scared, Tom. I'm so so scared.

Tom: I know. I know. (*She puts her head on his chest. Beat*) Me too. Me too.

Susan: And I know he's scared, and I want to hold him.

Tom: Me too. (*Long pause*) It's gonna be OK.

Beat.

Susan: Yeah?

Tom: Yeah.

Susan: Yeah. It's gonna be OK. (*Beat*) Promise?

Tom: Promise.

Susan: OK.

Tom: You promise me?

Susan: Yeah.

Tom: Then it's OK.

Susan: Find him for me, Tommy. Please. Find him for me and bring him home.

Tom: I will do that. (*They kiss*) I'm gonna go up there tomorrow, I've decided. I can't sit no more.

Susan: Good. Go. Please. (*Beat*) I'm tired.

Tom: Let's go to bed. C'mon, let's go. We're not making anything happen like this.

Susan: OK. Alright.

She looks around helplessly. Beat.

Tom: Come on, baby, let's go.

She nods. He take a pace towards the table to pick up the place settings.

Susan: No.

Beat.

Tom: Alright. OK.

They leave. Spotlight on the three place settings. Blackout.

Scene Two

Hanna Schneider, mid forties, at home, upstate New York. She holds a cellphone.

Hanna: I never knew that grief feels so much like fear.

I feel afraid. Butterflies in the stomach. I don't like the lights off at night and I don't like them on.

Or maybe I am, just, simply, afraid. Maybe there's no grief at all. The worst thing possible has already happened, and yet I'm terrified, of leaves against the window panes, noises on the stair, like a child.

Pause.

I try to read. People have sent me poetry. They tell me it's of great comfort. The words flow off my skin like oil.

Pause.

I took back your new winter coat. Tried to, anyway. They wouldn't give me a refund. They said "under exceptional circumstances only."

Flaherty's put up the 'God Bless America' like everybody else, but they didn't take down the old sign, so now it says: "God Bless America: 12 Bud for $8.99"

I thought you'd like that.

Flags everywhere. Little clusters of them poking out like spring flowers. As if something really great had happened, and everybody wanted to celebrate.

I lie down and I feel like getting up.

I get up, I feel like lying down.

Pause.

I carry this (*phone*) with me everywhere. Even into the shower. (*Bitter irony*) So I don't miss you this time.

I don't feel. It's too big to feel. I constantly expect you to call. I'm angry when the phone rings and it's not you. I'm angry at them for not being you.

She looks at the phone for a while. It remains mute.

I'm ashamed, Al. It doesn't hurt. It's too big to hurt. I'm like a word with all the letters taken out.

(*with piercing wonder*) Where are you? Why aren't you here?

She plays his last, ordinary message to herself one more time. Beat. Resolute.

I can't keep talking to you like this. I can't keep listening to this.
I'm gonna say goodbye now, my darling, alright?
I'm sorry, honey.
I'm gonna go now.
Bye.

Bye.

She deletes the message. Blackout.

Scene Three

The low sound of distant bombings and explosions, out of which rise news commentaries on the invasion of Afghanistan, referencing the start of "Operation Enduring Freedom." Bush: "We will not relent til justice is done."

Three weeks later. Tom and Susan at the table, close to each other. With them are their friends Ray and Sophia Villapiano. All four of them stare at a tiny white enamel box, made all the smaller by the expanse of empty table on which it sits. Long pause.

Ray: Are they sure?

Sophia: Ray.

Ray: Alls I'm asking is how can they be sure?

Sophia: They have tests.

Ray: They can't get tests wrong? They can get anything wrong, these people.

Beat.

Sophia: That's true, Susie.

Ray: Three years in a row they get my taxes wrong, these assholes. Whaddya trust 'em with? A month they don't collect the garbage. I gotta drive it to the dump myself.

Sophia: It's hardly the same thing, garbage and taxes.

Ray: Alls I'm saying is how can you be sure they got it right? With the pressure they're under? With, and I don't mean to make this a relative thing, because by God we know it's not a relative thing, but with the number of people we're talking about? They can't make a mistake?

Beat.

Susan: (*to Tom*) Maybe he's right. (*Tom looks at her. She shrugs a little painful shrug of wanted hope*) They can get DNA tests wrong, like anything else.

Sophia: It's not a big enough sample.

Susan: It's not enough

Ray: It don't *prove* it.

Susan: A piece the size of a quarter from his shoulder blade is not enough.

Pause.

Ray: All this time and that's all they can come up with, these fuckin people? C'mon, Tommy.

Sophia: There's always a possibility. There's always a possibility of something good.

Ray: Why not? Because a 'science'? Fuck science. They said it was scientifically impossible for the fuckin things to come down, and look where that got us.

Beat. Sophia takes Susan's hand.

Sophia: You don't do nothing the next few weeks, my darling, OK? The girls got a rota drawn up. There'll be somebody here every day. Cooking, cleaning, whatever, it's taken care of. So don't you worry about nothing.

Susan: Thank you.

Sophia: Whatever you need. I know you don't think so much of my cooking and I never done that cordon blue stuff you like to do—

Susan: I never said—

Sophia: But you're not alone, nohow. We're gonna take good care a that.

Susan: Thank you, Sophia.

Sophia: It's the least thing, my darling. The very leastest thing. And you know what else? I'm gonna take you to my art class.

Ray: (*to Tom, slightly surprised*) This art, she's real good, you know?

Susan: I don't know, Soph, I'm not—

Sophia: You kidding me? You have gorgeous taste. And doing art, it's so good for ya, Susie. This beautiful thing appears from somewhere inside a you, turns up right there between your hands. It's inspiring. (*Beat. She squeezes Susan's hand again*) I'm taking ya and that is that.

Pause.

Ray: You see they got more of them today, Tommy? Over there in… Oooga Booga Land. Got a whole lot more of them today. (*He smacks his fist into his other hand*) They're wrapping 'em up here, too. Pulling 'em all in. Nighty night, assholes. (*Beat*) Hey, Tommy, you remember that time? You remember that time when Eddie was what, freshman, soph maybe, and we caught that group of older kids picking on him? Tommy, he was outta the truck like he had Semtex between his ass cheeks, and he takes the biggest kid and damn near rips his head off.

Sophia: Ray.

Ray: Woulda spread that kid over three counties if I'da let him.

Sophia: (*gesturing furtively at the box on the table*) Ray!

Ray: What? I'm sorry, but…but this is the nature of this man here. This man who I am proud, who I am honoured to call my friend. This man does not take bullies. This man does not take cowards. This is a man goes into burning fuckin buildings to save the lives of people he don't even know, people don't even thank him, because it's the right thing to do and someone needs to do it and he does it. This is not right, and if it is even the case and we don't know for sure and God forbid. But it is not right. It is not right. It is *not right*. It ain't right on him and it ain't right on you either, Susie.

Susan: Thank you, Ray.

Ray: Because we are decent people. We are good people and we are open people and we let anybody in here as long as they wanna work hard, and then they do this to us, these cocksucking motherfucking cowards? No no no. Uh uh. Not to us. Not to people who do what we do. Not to people that run up inside buildings to save others and they don't come out again. Not to people that pull down planes they're inside so's other people don't get hurt. I hope they level that fucking place, Aphaganastan, I hope they crush every living thing in it now and forever. I hope they pound it so flat you can roll a quarter along it and it won't never stop rolling til it hits the horizon. And I am not a man that hates, you know? I don't hate nobody.

Beat.

Sophia: Patriots fans you hate.

Ray: Yeah, but Patriots fans, that's a different story. I'm talking about human beings here.

He grins at Tom, looking for a reaction. He doesn't get one. The women smile a bit. Ray leans forward to get through to Tom.

Tommy, listen. Now this don't contradict what I said before, because I don't happen to believe that science knows its ass from its elbow and there's plenty of time yet for something good to happen.

Sophia: People are coming back to their families all the time now. They got a knock on the head, they're confused, they don't know where they've been…

Ray: But if it comes to…Look, I had a talk with the super and he had a talk with whoever…You know they're gonna do a big commemoration up there at St Ignatius, for all the guys the fire department lost, across the region? Well, it looks like… They're gonna let Eddie be a part of that, Tom.

Sophia: Isn't it incredible?

Ray: They wouldn't normally do a thing like that, the super says, but this ain't anything but normal, I says, and he goes away and he comes back...

Sophia: Isn't it the kindest thing?

Ray: And he says it's a fireman's son and they should do for a fireman's son what they would do for a fireman.

Susan: I can't believe that they would do that.

Ray: I never pumped nobody's hand the way I pumped that son of a bitch's.

Susan: I can't believe you've done that for us, Ray. *Thank you.* Thank you.

Ray: I'm his godfather, Susie. Least I could do.

Susan: (*to Tom*) Do you hear this?

Sophia: It's good, Tommy, huh?

Susan: Do you hear this, honey? (*Beat*) Tom?

Pause.

Tom: They ain't cowards, anyway.

Ray: Who?

Tom: The people that done this. They ain't cowards.

Susan: What are you talking about them for?

Tom: I been up there and I seen it and they ain't cowards, those people. They ain't cowards and they didn't do it by accident. I seen it and that is a thing somebody really wanted to do.

Beat.

Susan: (*incredulous*) What are you talking about them for?

Tom: I wanna know why, Susie.

Susan: I don't wanna hear about them.

Tom: I wanna know why our son is dead.

Susan: I don't see how you can just *accept* that.

Tom: I wanna go back and back and understand why. A thing like that, it don't happen by accident. Our son is dead—

Susan: Don't say that!

Tom: …and I don't know why.

Beat.

Ray: We know why, kid

Tom: Do we, Ray?

Beat.

Ray: Whaddya mean, do we? Sure we do. These cunts, I'm sorry ladies but—

Susan: Oh, it's fine, Ray.

Ray: These murderers, they hate us, they flew—

Tom: Why do they hate us, Ray?

Ray: *I* don't fucking know.

Tom: Nor do I.

Ray: Ain't it obvious?

Tom: Not to me.

Susan: Tom.

Ray: The freedom, the choices we got, how the fuck would I know? I look like a fundamentalist to you?

Tom: Where'd you get that? That they hate us? From the government?

Ray: Jesus, Tommy, it's me here, OK?

Tom: Government tell you that?

Susan: Maybe from the fact that they flew planes into buildings full of people.

Tom: The people who don't pick up your garbage? The people who fuck up your taxes, who can't even bring the right body back to us? You trust 'em on this? You take their word for it?

Pause. Ray looks wounded.

Sophia: He's upset.

Susan: Did you hear what Ray did for us?

Tom: (*wounded*) There are things I don't understand here, Susie. About why this happened. About how this happened. I just don't understand what is going on here. (*Beat*) I got a quarter-sized piece of my son in that box there and the question is why.

He stares at the box. Susan shifts imperceptibly away from him. There is now a visible gap between the three of them and Tom. Pause. Tom stares at the box.

Sophia: (*squeezing Susan's arm*) Art class.

Blackout.

Scene Four

Central Park Zoo. Sunny day. Hanna on the grass with her husband's sister, Linda. Pause.

Linda: Such a beautiful day.

Hanna: Yes it is.

Linda: So beautiful. I *love* how so many of us are out here having a good time. Like, we are *determined* to have a good time. We won't let anyone intimidate us, or scare us away. "Here we are. Central Park. New York City. Having a good time. What are you gonna do about it? "

Beat.

Hanna: Mmmm.

Linda: It's been so beautiful almost every day since…well, since… Don't you think that's kinda, somehow, ironic? (*Pause*) The monkeys were great.

Hanna: Yeah, they were

Linda: I loved the little ones, what were they? The tamarinds?

Hanna: Uh-huh.

Linda: The way they come up to you, with their little human faces. They climb up your leg if you let them.

Hanna: I was with you. I saw them.

Linda: Their little faces. So human and yet so…monkey. And when the daddy pooped on the mommy? (*She laughs*) Men are the same all throughout the animal kingdom. I brought something nice. Close your eyes.

Hanna: Linda…

Linda: Close your eyes. (*Hanna closes them. A park attendant enters, picking up rubbish with a stick. Linda digs into her huge expensive handbag and pulls out a bottle of white wine and two glasses and places them in front of Hanna*) Here we go. Oh, sorry: you can open them now.

Hanna opens her eyes. She jumps at seeing the attendant near them and pulls back.

Linda: What's wrong?

Hanna: Nothing.

Linda: It's just a guy. Like a cleaner or something.

Hanna: I know that.

Linda: It's just a random guy, Hanna.

Hanna: I *know that*.

Linda: Well, come on then…

Hanna: (*sharp*) Come on *what*?

Beat.

Linda: C'mon and open up, I'd like a drink.

Beat. Hanna unscrews the bottle and pours two glasses. They drink and stare out front. Pause. Linda indicates the bag.

Linda: Did I show you this?

Hanna: Yeah.

Linda: Isn't it…?

Hanna: Yeah.

Linda: Isn't it? I know I shouldn't have. But it's been such a difficult time.

Hanna: Yes it has.

Linda: I just thought, "No, I deserve something. It's not the 'done thing' to admit it, to be honest with yourself, but I lost my brother and I deserve something." (*Beat*) What?

Hanna: I didn't say a thing.

Linda: Yes you did. Only without words. (*Beat*) I am *trying* to do something nice for you here.

Hanna: I know that. Thank you.

Linda: Then don't make me feel guilty, please.

Hanna: I… I'm just not very good company right now.

Beat.

Linda: You see, *I'm* not going to say anything, in case it makes you feel—

Hanna: Maybe we should go home.

Attendant: Excuse me, ladies?

Linda: Oh, I'm sorry, are we in your way? We can—

Attendant: No, I don't mean to bother you, I just wondered…Are you sisters?

Linda: (*smiling, putting her hand on Hanna's knee*) Yes.

(*simultaneously*)

Hanna: No.

Beat.

Hanna: In law. Sisters in law.

Attendant: It's just…from a distance you look like sisters. Like, real close.

Linda: (*warmly*) Thank you. That's a lovely thing to say. (*Beat*) We lost someone.

Attendant: I'm sorry?

Linda: In the…when the…? We lost someone. My brother. Her husband.

Attendant: I'm sorry to hear that.

Linda: Thank you. Maybe that's part of the reason we look like…

Both of them look at Hanna. She looks at the ground and fiddles with her glass. Beat.

Attendant: I lost someone that day too.

Linda: Oh my God, really? Who?

Attendant: Percy.

Linda: Percy? Was Percy your brother, your son—?

Attendant: Percy was a pot-bellied pig. Lived in the enclosure right over there. All the animals went crazy, screaming and honking and whatnot, and poor old Percy just had a heart attack. Boom. Dropped stone dead right at my feet.

Linda: Well, I'm…I'm very sorry to hear that.

Attendant: All the commotion, I guess it was just too much for him, you know? He was my favourite of all the pigs.

Beat.

Linda: And are they better now?

Attendant: Sorry?

Linda: The rest of the…pigs, the rest of the animals? They're better now?

Attendant: Ah yeah, they're back to normal now. Animals are pretty resilient, ya know? (*Beat*) Anyway, I better get on. Nice talking to yis.

He leaves. Linda guffaws.

Linda: Percy the pot-bellied pig?! You believe that guy?

Hanna: (*quietly*) He's not the only one, sis.

Linda: What? (*Beat*) What did you say to me?

Hanna: You weren't close to Al, Linda.

Linda: What did you just say to me?

Hanna: You weren't close to him. It's a statement of fact. In fact, you hated him.

Beat.

Linda: How dare you? How dare you, you snobby, snotty little... I'm *scared*, Hanna. I lost my brother and I'm scared. Why wouldn't I be scared? *People hate us.* Nobody can believe anything else now and we never will be able to. They hate us. Who knows who else is out there, what else they have in store for us, plots, bombs, the anthrax—

Hanna: Anthrax is not the same people.

Linda: What's it matter who it is, it's still anthrax, isn't it? You get it in the mail, what does it matter who sent it to you? This is what I mean. You look at people in the street, on the subway, and of course you look extra hard at the brown people *because the brown people did it,* and you wonder what that is in their eyes. Was that hate always there and you just didn't see it? Or is it new and they feel strong enough to hate us now because they got away with it? I feel stupid for all the kind things I did in the past for people. Because what did it serve? And I want to scare them, the brown people, I want to terrify them, because why should we be the only ones to be afraid? I want the President to bomb that side of the world so they can feel what we feel. And I take solace in the one solid thing there is after what I lost, the solidarity, the togetherness, and you rip it away with that sanctimonious little look on your face like you never did a thing wrong in your life.

Beat.

Hanna: I'm gonna volunteer in a soup kitchen at Ground Zero.

Linda slaps Hanna. Hanna pours her wine into Linda's open bag. Linda gasps, then leaves in tears. Hanna stares at the sky.

Hanna: You wanna explain to me how the only mortal shred left of you on this earth is *her*? You wanna explain that to me, Al, you sonofabitch? You goddamn worthless asshole sonofabitch? You wanna explain that to me, my beautiful darling?

She slowly dissolves into great wracking tears.

Scene Five

*A few weeks later. Radio static, talk show hosts cutting across one
another in their rage. Giuliani: "Freedom is about authority. Freedom
is about the willingness of every single human being to cede to lawful
authority a great deal of discretion about what you do and how you
do it."*

Tom in a studio with a radio shock jock, the Mad Dog.

Mad Dog: So what you're telling me, this cult of hate-fuelled,
puritanical, mass-murdering cocksuckers who believe they gotta *divine
obligation*—

Tom: What I'm saying is—

Mad Dog: To kill everyone who doesn't smell bad, stone their many
fucking wives and answer to the name 'Mohammed'—

Tom: It don't add up—

Mad Dog: These men, the scum who murdered your son in cold blood,
these sand niggers we should invade their countries, kill their leaders
and convert what's left to Christianity—

Tom: Listen, sir, it don't/ add up.

Mad Dog: That these—who we all *saw* do it—

Tom: I just want to know—

Mad Dog: Cos you do actually know what happened here, right? You
do have a TV? Mental institutions these days got TVs, right, if there's
still any open thanks to our liberal friends? So you did see what actually
happened?

Tom: I saw what was on *television*—

Mad Dog: That these men in fact *didn't* do it? Didn't do the thing
billions of people saw them do?

Tom: That's not what I'm saying.

Mad Dog: Then what are you sayin, Tommy boy?

Tom: What I'm saying—

Mad Dog: Cos I'm *all* fuckin ears here.

Tom: What I'm saying, I got questions—

Mad Dog: Oh, you got *questions*?

Tom: About—

Mad Dog: You don't got answers but you got questions? How fucking useful.

Tom: About what we're being told here, sir.

Mad Dog: You know what, Tommy? I got a question too.

Tom: Why didn't they scramble a single jet when the planes went/ off course?

Mad Dog: My question is: does Osama have a big thick cock, or one of those little stringy ones like yours?

Tom: Passenger planes go off course over New York City and they don't—

Mad Dog: Or d'you close your eyes when you suck him off so you don't know? Does he wash under his foreskin? That's another one. Or he make you lick it clean for him?

Tom: Pardon me?

Mad Dog: What's Osama's asshole taste like, Tommy?

Tom: What?

Mad Dog: What's Osama's special chocolate taste like, Tom? When he shits it in your mouth, all over your face—

Tom: You got no right—

Mad Dog: I got *every* fuckin right on *my* show—

Tom: I'm a Republican and I come on here to—

Mad Dog: You ain't a Republican, Tommy, you're the very farthest fucking thing from a Republican.

Tom: I used to love your show and I—

Mad Dog: There's only one word for you and the word is traitor.

Tom: I'm the biggest patriot here. I wanna find out what happened to my country.

Mad Dog: Trai-tor. Giving aid and comfort to the enemy. You're the fuckin raghead Benedict Arnold, Tommy boy! You know what they should do with guys like you? They should invent some place, way the fuck out there beyond all the activist judges and the liberal trial lawyers, some fucking place in like, I don't know, Cuba or some shit, where they can take guys like you and just torture them all day long because that is what you deserve, Tom, that is what you deserve!

Tom: My son died.

Mad Dog: And you shit on his grave, Thomas! You shit on his grave, you shanty Mick, sand nigger-loving, Benedict Arnold, faggot ass-licking treasonous cocksucker!

Tom: You—

Tom stands and is dragged away.

Mad Dog: Get the fuck away from me. Get the fuck outta here. You're a traitor to your country and a traitor to your son. Take care now! (*Beat*) Folks, unfortunately our guest had to leave us, but if any of you would like to carry on this discussion with Mr McFarlane in your own time, his number is 973, I believe that's a Paterson number for anyone passing through the neighbourhood and enjoying our constitutionally protected right to bear arms, let's see, 973 241 0573. Alright, fuck politics, time for some music. Keep it l-l-l-locked onto the Mad Dog! GRRRRR! We'll be right back.

He takes off his headphones and wipes his brow. To producer:

And that, my friend, is show business. (*Beat*) You know I almost felt sorry for the guy? (*Beat*) Fuck you Jacko, you're the faggot. You got a smoothie or something back there? My throat's a little tickly.

Blackout. Screaming phone ins: "It's crap like you that's killing America", "You know what we do to traitors here?" Lights up. Tom and Susan at home. Susan is playing answerphone messages: "You love these other countries so fucking much, whyn't you fucking move there?", etc. The last message is a drawn-out, sinister hiss, silence, then a loud bang. Susan flinches slightly. Silence. Pause.

Susan: When did you decide to do that?

Tom: You know what the worst thing was? None of them would say he died. We did a phone-in bit first and none of 'em called in would say he died. They'd all start up with this little apology, "I'm sorry about your son and shit, " and they was all sorry he 'passed' or he 'moved on' or we 'lost' him. Not a one of 'em could say the word.

Susan: When did you decide to do that, Thomas?

Beat.

Tom: The guy rang me a couple days ago, says he read my piece in the *Courier.*

Susan: Goddamn it, Tommy.

Tom: What?

Susan: He's "The Mad Dog." "Biting Out the Throats of Liberals, Weekdays from Nine to Midnight."

Tom: I ain't no liberal.

Susan: Evidently he doesn't agree.

Tom: The guy claims he wants to tell the truth. That's the whole pitch of the show, 'The Unvarnished Truth'. And then you tell the truth and—

Susan: Not everybody would agrees it's the truth, Tom. I'd go so far as to say the vast majority of people don't agree it's the truth. (*She taps the machine*) Thirty-seven messages. I get back from class, there's—

Tom: How is class?

Susan: Class is good.

Tom: What you working on?

Susan: A portrait of Eddie. *Do not* change the subject. Any idea what I thought might have happened when I saw thirty-seven messages on the answering machine? (*Pause*) A little glimmer of hope, a little flicker. You raised it and then you erased it, just like that. That was cruel. (*Beat*) No, please don't apologise.

Tom: I'm sorry, Susie, I—

Susan: Thirty-six of them, like you heard. Halfway through I have to stop the tape and lock the doors and draw all the curtains. Got my biggest knife out of the drawer.

Tom: I swear to God I had no idea the cocksucker would give out our number.

Susan: And the other one is from Eddie's landlord, asking for a month's rent.

Tom: Are you serious?

Susan: Normally it'd be three months, he says, if a tenant fails to give prior notice that he will no longer be needing the facility, but in view of the extenuating circumstances, he says, he's willing to knock it down to a month.

Tom: Knock it down? I'm gonna knock down that son of a bitch's—

Susan: I want you to stop using Eddie.

Pause.

Tom: What are you talking about?

Susan: You heard what I said.

Tom: I'm not 'using' Eddie.

Susan: Yes you are. You used him in your *Courier* piece. (*She reads*) "My son would not want his death to be used to inflict further suffering on innocent people."

Tom: And?

Susan: That is not what he thought.

Tom: Sure it—

Susan: It's what you think. Now it's one thing for you to do that show, to discuss ideas I profoundly disagree with—

Tom: These are things that need to be said, Susie.

Susan: ...and not to bother telling me—

Tom: You know how many warnings they had, the White House?

Susan: I'm a big girl—

Tom: From the FBI, from their own people?

Susan: I can put you on the couch for the night.

Tom: You know Bush had detailed warnings, in advance—

Susan: Make that the week.

Tom: …of attacks predicted the week of September 9th? Detailed warnings! This stuff is known! People won't see what's right up in front of their faces!

Susan: What gives *you* the right to judge them, Thomas?

Tom: Because they deserve to be judged! Because they are fucking cowards! Because they huddle together like sheep and then boast about being individuals! This administration tells them to preserve freedom we gotta take freedom away, and these people, these strong proud individual Americans, they roll over and they take it. And I try to exercise my God-given rights to find out what really went on that day and they tell me *I'm* the bad guy? Isn't that what a Republican government should be about, the rights of the individual? What these pieces of shit say they're about?

Susan: I don't know, you tell me. You voted for 'these pieces of shit'. I voted for the other guy. So tell me about these people you elected.

Beat.

Tom: Sal Grewal.

Susan: Who?

Tom: Sikh guy, beard and the whole shebang, lives over on Piedmont? Looks kinda like somebody else been on TV an awful lot lately.

Susan: I know him.

Tom: Put in a coma two days ago. Four guys with baseball bats beat the shit out of him.

Susan: That's wrong.

Tom: This is what is happening in this country now, Susie.

Susan: It's wrong, there's nothing else needs to be said.

Tom: Guy owns two liquor stores and the firing range. Can't get much more American than guns and liquor.

Susan: You take responsibility for yourself before you start lecturing others.

Tom: What is *that* supposed to mean?

Susan: Eddie is not here to defend himself and I will not let you—

Tom: Defend himself against who?

Susan: I am not gonna let you take him away again.

Beat.

Tom: I am trying to be true to what he was, to what *you* taught him to be, Sooz.

Susan: Eddie was a patriotic kid.

Tom: This is patriotic. This is what patriotism should be.

Susan: Eddie was a patriotic kid. What about that Reserve Officer Training Program you made him do his junior year?

Tom: That was a course, lasted a week—

Susan: He enjoyed that course.

Tom: Yes he did, for a week. And you hated him doing it! You chewed my ear off non-stop!

Susan: I am not—

Tom: 'Jingoistic nationalism', you called it, and a whole bunch of other words I didn't understand.

Susan: I am not the one using him.

Tom: I am not using him, Susan. If anyone is using him, it's these assholes wanna make a statue out of him, put him in the papers—

Susan: What's wrong with making a statue out of him? What's wrong with him being in the papers?

Tom: Not like this—

Susan: I like him being in the papers. He's still alive if he's in the papers.

Tom: Susie—

Susan: (*venomously*) Don't you call it weak! Don't you dare say I'm weak when you weren't strong enough to keep him around here! (*Beat*) You wanna argue it with me?

Beat.

Tom: I never wanted nothing but the best for my son.

Susan: Until his best was better than your best. Until he knew things you didn't know. Until he made you feel stupid and uneducated and ignorant.

Tom: Is that what you think of me, Susan?

Susan: No it's not, but it's what *you* think of you, my love, and that's what counts. And it's too late now, Tom. It's too late to make up for it by studying up about Islam and flight patterns.

Tom: That is not why I'm doing this.

Susan: It's too late to make up for it and it's too late to apologise. Especially in this strange twisted horrible way.

Tom: I do not owe anyone an apology.

Susan: Oh, I think you do. I think you do.

Tom: I am trying to do the best by my son. I am trying to find out who killed him, and why, and what that means. I want my son's death to mean what it really means.

Susan: You don't get to decide. You don't get to decide what something means.

Tom: Then who does? He was *my son*. Everything is slipping away here, Susie. Everything is going faster and faster in the wrong direction.

Susan: It's slipping away because you're taking it, Tom! You're pulling everything away from me and I want it back. I can't lose anything more now, I can't! Why isn't it enough for you, what we know? It's enough for everybody else, why isn't it enough for you?

Beat.

Tom: I just want to know the truth.

Susan: What about the truth about us?

Blackout.

Scene Six

Diane: Isn't it about time people heard your side of the story?

Lights up. Susan in the office of a senior New Jersey Republican congresswoman, Diane Roberts. Sophia off to one side. Pause.

The story of someone who has truly suffered. Who knows at the deepest, most personal level what the true cost of terrorism is. Who knows in the depths of her heart why vigilance is necessary, why it will always be necessary. Isn't somebody like that the kind of woman America really needs to hear from right now? (*Pause*) You sure I can't get you a drink, Susan? Something to eat?

Susan: I'm fine, thank you.

Diane: I mean, the first thing I thought when Sophia approached me about this, and I'm very glad she did—

Sophia: You're welcome, Senator.

Diane: (*smiling at Sophia*) Congresswoman.

Sophia: Oh, I'm sorry.

Diane: No problem. I thought—

Sophia: I mean, they're both good, right? Senate, Congress? They're both great, y'know? And real important, Susie.

Diane: Thank you, Sophia. I thought, "I really want to hear what this woman has to say. We all *think* we know what this means: she *knows* what this means. Truly *knows* it. We have a *responsibility* to hear what this woman thinks."

Susan: I'm a Democrat.

Sophia: And you should enjoy to be part of the majority for once.

Susan: We were. At the last election.

Diane: (*smiling*) I don't wanna make this a political thing, Susan. Something this important should be above politics. (*Beat*) I understand. It's a big deal, at a difficult time, and that's why I'd be more than happy to share the speaking duties with you. If you'd prefer, I'll shoulder the load and you can just chip in with whatever you feel comfortable with.

Susan: I don't even know who's going to be speaking.

Diane: Well, that's surely up to you, isn't it? You're the mother.

Beat.

Sophia: I think it'd be good, Susie.

Susan: I don't know if I wanna use Eddie like that.

Diane: I wouldn't see it as—

Sophia: Tommy is.

Diane: Sophia, maybe—

Sophia: He is though! He's on the radio talking about how he hates the government and Eddie would too!

Susan: He's not doing that.

Diane: I don't think it's helpful—

Sophia: He's on the radio and in the papers too!

Diane: I don't think you should think of it as 'using' Eddie, certainly not in any negative way. I think if anything, you'd be doing quite the opposite. I think you'd be *honouring* Eddie: what he was, what he meant to his family and friends and his community. From what everyone tells me of your son, you should be very proud of him, and if there's one thing we need right now, it is to be proud. To be confident and strong and not to believe what the terrorists would like us to believe, that we deserve what happened. I don't believe you deserve what happened to your son, Susan.

Sophia: And I don't either. .

Diane: I think you can do something for all of us by honouring your son for what he was, a free and proud and good American. We need that right now. This country, this community, we need that. And I imagine you need that too. Don't you?

Pause.

Susan: Yeah.

Diane: Then do something for us, Susan, and let us do something for you. Together, we can make Eddie's death mean something good.

Pause. Blackout.

Scene Seven

Hanna behind the counter at the soup kitchen near Ground Zero. Enter Jessica, a British tourist on her mobile phone.

Jessica: No, frankly, it's rubbish. Because it's essentially a bloody great pile of rubble, which regardless of its momentous socio-political importance does become just a tad dull after a while. But of course you can't *say* that, you have to go around doing the mourning face and nodding sombrely when you meet someone's gaze… (*Looks around*) I mean, fair dos, obviously it's a horrible trauma for those concerned, although you're not even allowed to say *that*, you must refer to it on pain of death as "the tragedy of 9/11", you are literally not *allowed* to use the term '9/11' without affixing 'tragedy' to the front of it or you'll be excommunicated or deported to Guantanamo, depending on your religious beliefs…(*Beat*) I'm not being callous, no. If you were here, Fi…If you were here…The way they gawk and stare, these pastel-clothed pachyderms from Buttfuck Indiana in their gormless little clumps. D'you remember when we went to Rome, the absolute *reverence* in some of those churches? Well, it's like that here, with the unwelcome addition that they all think they're Jesus into the bargain. They *do* though, darling. They *love* it. They've been wanting to feel like victims for *so* long and now finally they can. Hold on one second. (*to Hanna*) Could I get a bowl of soup, please?

Hanna: We don't—

Jessica: The chicken, please. Large.

She turns her back to Hanna and resumes her conversation.

Hanna: This is for workers and volunteers only. It's not for—

Jessica: I mean, don't get me wrong, I have tried to feel, you know, the appropriate sadness etc etc…But all the kitsch, Fi, all the endless flags and poetry and the saccharine pledges to honour the lost because they were a gift from the great creator, the whole way they go on like nothing bad ever happened to anyone else before, it just… it sticks in the craw. Not to mention the people flogging pictures of the towers exploding. I mean, what is *that*? I don't remember anyone selling snapshots of Auschwitz in 1945, do you? Sorry, darling, I've been holding it in for three days… (*Suddenly serious*) You watch though. You watch what this makes Blair do. You watch what Britain does after this, what it lets us sanction. You see if I'm not entitled to a wee bit of cynicism. (*to Hanna*) I ordered a chicken soup? (*Back to call*) No, but really and truly, Fiona, what did they expect? It was only a matter of time. That *is* what I'm saying. They *did* have it coming. (*Beat*) Anyway, I've done my duty, I'm having a quick spot of lunch and then I'm off to Bloomie's. Now, what was it you wanted again? Donna Karan—

Hanna reaches over, grabs Jessica's mobile and drops it into a vat of soup.

Hanna: Fuck. Off. Back. Home.

Jessica is flabbergasted. Pause.

Jessica: You see, this is my point entirely. You people can't take the simplest bit of criticism.

Scene Eight

The commemoration ceremony in a large Jersey church. The hum of conversation and the sense of a very large and warm gathering of people. The stone is draped in a huge Stars and Stripes that bears the prominent legend "These Colors Don't Run." Susan stands with Ray and Sophia, as well as Diane. All of them are dressed formally. Susan keeps checking her watch and looking anxiously towards the door.

Sophia: It's so exciting!

Susan: Yeah.

Diane: It's a very impressive turnout.

Sophia: The whole neighbourhood is here!

Ray: And all these bigshots…Listen, Congresswoman—

Diane: Diane.

Ray: Yeah. You got—

Sophia: Isn't that the Carmazzis? Yoo-hoo, Jenny! *Jenny!*

Ray: Keep it down to a dull roar, Soph, heh? There's big people here.

Sophia: Raymond, live a little…

Ray: (*to Diane*) You got like secret service people out there? Federal agents and whatnot?

Diane: The mayor's office has deployed appropriate security personnel, yes.

Sophia: (*to Susan*) Are you nervous?

Susan: A little.

Ray: Like in case of snipers or some such?

Diane: Snipers?

Sophia: Cos I would be nervous. In front of all these people?

Susan: OK, a lot.

Ray: You gotta take the possibility into account, you know?

Sophia: I would be *so* nervous.

Diane: I don't think snipers—

Ray: These are crazy times, Ms Diane, there's some crazy people out there right now. You gotta take the possibility into account.

Sophia: And with *Rudy* coming?

Ray: I'm just worried about Susie's welfare here.

Sophia: (*to Diane*) Is that true? Is Rudy really going to come?

Diane: I know Mayor Giuliani has the ceremony on his schedule for today—

Sophia: (*grabbing Susan's arm*) *Rudy's* coming! Can you believe it?

Susan: (*looking out the door*) That's great, Soph.

Enter Tom, in a new suit. Susan visibly relaxes. He stares at the group. Long pause. Ray strides over to him.

Ray: Wasn't sure you were gonna make it today.

Tom: It's for my son. Why wouldn't I be here?

Beat. Ray extends a hand. Beat. Tom shakes it.

Ray: Yeah, well it's good to see you, asshole.

Tom: Yeah?

Ray: Fuck you think? Oops.(*Remembers where they are and claps his hand over his mouth*) Remember how old McGinley useta get on me about profanity in the fuckin church? Oops. (*Tom says nothing but smiles slightly at the memory. Beat*) Of course it's good to see you, Tommy. Look at you. Is that a new suit?

Tom: Yeah. (*Beat*) How'm I looking?

Ray: Like you never wore one before in your life. Get over here. (*He straightens Tom's tie*) All the funerals we been to and you never learned to tie one of these things.

Tom: That new too? I didn't see it before.

Ray: My father's. I save it for special occasions.

Beat.

Tom: It's good to see you, Ray.

Ray: You too, buddy. This here is for you today. All for you. (*Pointing at the flag*) You know we bought that?

Tom: (*trying to hide his distaste*) Yeah?

Ray: Bought an even bigger one originally, but she (*jerks thumb at Sophia*) got chocolate on it and when we washed it, it got all streaked up.

Tom: I guess those colours did run.

Ray: Fuckin Taiwanese piece a shit (*claps hand to mouth again*). It's good, though, huh? The portrait?

Tom: You seen it?

Ray: Sure!

Tom: She wouldn't let me see it.

Susan moves to them. Ray nods and respectfully drops back to join the rest. Pause.

Susan: Nice suit.

Tom: Thanks. Found it on the couch last night. Fits just right. Someone must be looking after me.

Susan: I guess so. (*Beat*) Wasn't sure you were going to make it.

Tom: That's what Ray said too. You all got the same script?

Susan: Where'd you go this morning?

Beat.

Tom: Driving around. Thinking about things. Me and Eddie. About how...(*Beat*) I wish it was just us two here, Susie..

Susan: Tom—

Tom: If it was just us two we could work it out, you know?

Susan: I want you to try and understand why I'm doing this today. Who this is for. OK? Please. I need you to set aside what *you* think, what you feel, and try to understand what I'm doing here, and for whom. Capisce?

Tom: (*slight smile*) I hate it when you try to do Jersey.

Susan: (*parody*) Whaddyayougonnadoaboutit? (*Beat*) Please, Tom.

Beat.

Tom: I'll try, Susie.

The sound of organ music and the hum of conversation drops away. Diane mounts the pulpit by climbing onto the cart. The rest sit and listen.

Diane: September 11 2001 will always be the defining moment of modern America. We have resolved to honour every last person lost. We owe them remembrance. And we owe them something far greater, the most enduring monument we can build: we owe them a world of liberty and security made possible by the way America leads in the world, and by the way Americans lead our lives.

The attack on our nation was also an attack on the ideals that make us a nation. Our deepest national conviction is that every life is precious, because every life is the gift of a creator who intended us to live in liberty and equality. More than anything else, this separates us from the enemy we fight. We value every life. Our enemies value none - not even the innocent, not even their own.

Murmurs of agreement from the crowd.

Tom: (*muttering*) Jesus Christ...

Diane: I believe there is a reason that history has matched this nation with this time. I believe that God has placed us together in this moment, to grieve together, to stand together, to serve each other and our country. We have been given a privilege: to defend America and our freedom. And with that privilege comes responsibility: not to waver, not to doubt, to remain, above all, unified.

Louder crowd noises.

Ray: That's right. That is right.

Tom: (*louder than he intended*) Bullshit.

Heads turn and look at him.

Diane: This nation has defeated tyrants and fought for freedom in every captive land. We have no intention of appeasing history's latest gang of fanatics trying to murder their way to power. They are discovering, as others before them, the resolve of this great country and this great democracy. In the ruins of two towers, we have made a sacred promise, to ourselves and to the world: we will not relent until justice is done and our nation is secure. What our enemies have begun, we will finish.

Louder agreement from the crowd: a baying. Someone at the back shouts "These Colors Don't Run!"

Tom: Jesus fuckin Christ....

Diane: Now, if you'd please like to stand with me and acknowledge a remarkable woman, a woman who epitomises the best of America, a dignity and honour in the face of loss from which we can all draw inspiration...Susan Macfarlane.

Susan rises. The crows applauds loudly. Susan makes her way up to the front. Diane steps down from the podium to allow Susan to step in. She enters, turns shyly to the audience, takes them in for a second.

Susan: Thank you all so much for coming here today. This is my son Eddie.

She wrenches away the flag to reveal a portrait she has painted: Eddie in the military uniform of the Reserve Officer Training Corps.

Tom: (*instinctively*) No.

Susan: My son Eddie was everything I wanted him to be. He was brave. He was generous and kind. And he was proud of his country.

Tom: (*rising*) That is not him!

Ray: What are you—

Tom starts to push his way to the front. Ray and Sophia restrain him.

Tom: That is not my son!

Diane: You can't come up here.

Tom: You lying motherfucker. You *lying* motherfucker.

Diane: How dare—

Tom: You value every life? You lying motherfucker.

He spits in Diane's face. She cries out and falls back. The crowd roars in anger.

Ray: Get the fuck back here. Spit in a woman's—?

Tom: (*to Susan*) What are you doing?

Susan: I told you.

Tom: What are you *doing*?

Susan: I *told* you. You dumb… I *told* you to try—

Tom: THAT IS NOT MY SON.

He makes a lunging grab for the painting of Eddie, trying to rip it down with his clawed hands. The crowd roars. Ray and the others wrestle him away, all swearing and shouting, and form a knot in front of the picture. Tom faces them alone. Pause.

Tom: Cowards.

Ray: Get outta here.

Tom: Gutless fucking cowards. Look at you. You're like fish huddled together when the shark comes, hoping and praying he'll take someone else.

Diane: It's only for your wife and son that I haven't let security beat you to a pulp. Get out of here.

Tom: So's you can sell my kid's bones for bombs to kill someone else? Fuck you, lady.

Ray: You keep talking like that, you'll cause the next one.

Tom: Cowards.

Sophia: (*exploding*) Stop saying that! I am afraid. Yes. I am. So what, Tom? I gotta reason, don't I? You of all people should know that.

Tom: Oh, I know.

Sophia: I have to protect my children.

The chanting rises and rises: "These Colors Don't Run." "These Colors Don't Run." "These Colors Don't Run."

Tom: Like they protected mine? These cocksuckers (*pointing at Diane*) killed my son! They knew it was coming and they let it happen and they killed my son! And now they wanna *profit* from that? I will not allow—

Susan: You killed your son, Thomas. You killed him. (*Sudden silence. Pause*) Yes you did. They couldn't have killed him without what you did so you're just as much to blame. (*Beat*) Go ahead and argue it, but in your hearts of hearts you know it's true.

Beat.

Tom: It's not true, Susie.

Susan: You *scared* him. You pushed him away. You pushed him out of our house.

Tom: I loved him.

Susan: You pushed and banged and hammered on him so much he came to hate you. You drove him out of the house and far away and that is how he came to be in that place to die. You killed him, Tom. (*Beat*) Go, Thomas. Go away.

They huddle closer. The chanting resumes. The lights slowly contract to a single spotlight on Tom. Blackout.

Interval.

Act Two

Scene One

June 2003. A long steep hill in rural Connecticut. The sound of birds and the occasional passing car. Flowers. Sunshine.

Tom and Hanna slumped on the ground, sweating and breathing heavily and leaning against the cart for support, having just pulled it up the hill. Pause.

Tom: Where d'you live, Hanna?

Hanna: Upstate New York. Ithaca.

Tom: Sure, I know it. Whaddya do?

Hanna: Music therapist, singing therapy. Or I did.

Tom: What happened, they let you go?

Hanna: No, I lost it. I had perfect pitch all my life and then afterwards, I lost it. Overnight. What use is a music teacher with no pitch? And the weirdest thing is I don't even know that I've lost it. When I sing it still sounds perfect to me. It's only the looks on people's faces that tell me otherwise. Listen. (*She runs through an arpeggio and gets it painfully wrong. Tom winces. She laughs ruefully*) You see!

Tom: What? Sounded great to me.

Hanna: You're sweet.

Tom: Don't make me sing, you'll get every dog in the neighbourhood howling. Those PETA people'll come round and pour red paint over me for cruelty to animals. (*Beat*) You enjoying this?

Hanna: Sure.

Tom: It doesn't seem a little, I don't know, a little passive to you?

Hanna: Passive?

Tom: Like we should be doing something more, you know, something…(*he smacks a fist into his other hand*).

Hanna: You call pulling a huge rock from Boston to New York City in the heat of summer passive?

Tom: That prick is walking around talking about "Mission Accomplished" and we're out here in the boondocks.

Hanna: I guess your definition of passive is a little different from mine.

Tom: I don't see how it hurts 'em, you know?

Hanna: Who says we wanna hurt them?

Tom: You don't wanna hurt the people that done this to you? (*She looks at him. Pause*) You hear those assholes back there? "Four more years", "four more years"… Retards. And that's the fuckin *police*? Gives you a ton of confidence.

Hanna: Tom.

Tom: What?

Hanna: Listen.

They listen for a moment.

Tom: I don't hear nothing.

Hanna: That would be my point.

Beat.

Tom: Aaah, I don't like when it's too quiet. I don't trust it, you know?

Hanna: You don't trust what?

Tom: I dunno. "*Nature*".

Hanna: Just listen.

Pause. Tom tries to restrain himself but can't—when did he last get to talk to someone who'd listen?

Tom: This was my country and now it ain't. I don't know when that flipped over. My dad, he used to say he could date it to the day, to the war. He was a blue-collar guy, stevedore on the docks. Skilled guy, vested. He voted Democrat all his life and he taught me to be proud to do three things: to work, to be American, and to fuck the bosses. And then Vietnam came and there wasn't no work and the Democrats stopped being proud to be American and they stopped being proud to fuck the bosses. And I thought, "At least the Republicans do *one* of 'em. At least they believe in *something*."

Pause.

When I first joined the department they had us on these demonstrations, you know, anti-war stuff, in case the demonstrators set fire to themselves like they seen that Buddhist guy do on TV. I mean, this is not why I joined, right? Buildings do not set themselves on fire. It is not the fault of a building, it catches fire. People, they have a choice. And we're standing around waiting for one of these intellectuals to make best use of his fifty thousand dollar education by making like Quaker State, and I spot this piece of graffiti on the wall: "Plastic Bullets, Kill and Maim!" And I honestly thought it was, like, *encouragement*, you know? 'Go plastic bullets!' Because what the fuck else is a bullet supposed to do? You don't want a bullet to kill and maim, use a fuckin ping-pong ball, a feather, something. (*Beat*) I see those cocksuckers on the TV, smirking into the camera, talking about "Mission Accomplished", that graffiti comes back into my head. Kill and maim. (*Beat*) I met my wife on that demonstration. She was trying to start something and I was trying to stop it.

Pause. Hanna is increasingly irked.

Hanna: (*arch*) That's a lovely story. Apart from the entire 'Kill and maim' part.

Tom: Can I tell you something?

Hanna: No, actually.

Tom: Every time the cart goes over a rock I imagine it's one of their skulls. Bush. Cheney. Wolfowitz. Rove. Every time a branch snaps under the wheels I dream it's their spinal cords. The people that let my son die. I want to line them up, all of them, their wives, their little slutty daughters, and I want to crush them screaming to death. Their bile smeared on the roadside like oil. Their bones ground and cracked and their blood tainting the puddles. I want them to know what is going to happen to them before it happens. Unendurable misery and everlasting pain.

Hanna stares at him. Abruptly she grabs her rucksack from the back of the cart and storms out. A moment or two later she storms back in, throws her bag back into the cart and rummages through the other bags.

Hanna: Which one of these is yours?

Tom: What?

Hanna: The fuck am *I* doing leaving? Which one of these is yours?

Tom: The red one. (*She finds it and throws it at him*) What?

Hanna: Get the fuck away from here.

Tom: Why?

Hanna: Get away from here. Go. There are (*checks watch*) seven more minutes before the rest of them come back and I want to enjoy those seven minutes in peace. Go. (*Beat*) *Go.* You don't deserve to be on this thing.

Beat.

Tom: I ain't going anywhere, lady.

Hanna: People give us soup out here.

Tom: It was good soup.

Hanna: They gave us soup back there!

Tom: I said thank you.

Hanna: How *dare* you make me swallow that *bile*?

Tom: It's the truth.

Hanna: The truth. The truth does not exempt you, pal. The truth is not some get-out-of-jail-free card that lets you say and do any fucking thing you want. Isn't that your point about Bush?

Tom: They don't tell the truth. I do.

Hanna: (*pointing at the stone*) You read that? You read that thing we've been pulling all this time?

Tom: Yeah, I read that. It's why I'm here.

Hanna: Is it? To talk about death and murder and plastic fucking bullets?! That your idea of a fucking memorial?

Tom: It's what needs to be said.

Hanna: There is *no space*! There is no space in this country! There is no oxygen to just breathe, every breath you get is blown down your throat by somebody pro-war, anti-war—

Tom: You think there's a *balance*? 'Pro-war', 'anti-war', there's some kinda '*balance*', like they don't have every TV station, every newspaper—?

Hanna: I don't give a shit!

Tom: There's no balance! There is right and there is wrong!

Hanna: I am just trying to breathe here! I am just trying to get some space to be...not even to be me, no, shit, anything but me. I'm sick of me. I'm bored shitless of grief, its rhythms and swoons and twisted ecstasies. I bore myself to tears. I want to be somebody else.

Tom: I didn't—

Hanna: I have been travelling around for two years, thinking it was only wherever I was that the oxygen was polluted, that as soon as I got on to the next place I'd be able to catch my breath and work out who I was, and then it'd be the next place, and the next... And finally I manage to get myself here, and people give you soup and you have a purpose, something to do every day, you can't get a much clearer purpose than pulling a big fucking *rock* from A to B, and I can start to breathe, to gasp for real air—and you come and you smother me again. It's not right. I tried to listen to you because, believe me, I know where all that comes from, but you must know it's not right, Tom.

Pause.

Tom: I'm sorry. (*She shrugs. Beat*) This is the best thing to happen to me in two years. To take everything and crush it under sheer physical pain, grind it, bury it, dissolve it in sweat and piss...I could push this thing all night if they'd let me.

Hanna: I'm ecstatic for you.

Tom: Please don't make me leave here.

Hanna: I can't *make* you leave here.

Tom: I like it here.

Hanna: You do whatever you wanna do. (*Acid*) It's a free country, right?

Beat. He just stands there with his bag in his hand. She takes it from him and throws it in the back of the cart, then moves away. He sits down heavily. Long pause.

Tom: I don't have a single picture of him and me after he was fifteen years old. When I moved out I looked everywhere for one, to take with me, and I thought she'd hidden them from me…and I went crazy, and I screamed at her…and I made her show me all the albums, every picture…and there was nothing. Of me and him after fifteen years of age, there was nothing. All there was, him and her, him and his friends, him and his girl. And he could be a little asshole, don't get me wrong, a sanctimonious little prick when he felt like it. He rubbed his education in my face like all my years in the force weren't worth his college intro to Marx. But he was a child and I was a man and it is unforgivable. It is unforgivable. And I don't know what's worse: that there are no pictures, or that I didn't even know there are no pictures.

Pause.

Hanna: Don't do that to yourself. (*Beat*) There's no point—

Tom: It's only because he died that I know there's no pictures. Why do we always think there's time? There's never time. There's *never* time, Hanna. If he was alive today, there'd still be no pictures of me and him after fifteen. I'd still be catching his mom slamming the receiver down guiltily like she was cheating on me with our own kid…Who'd I think I was punishing? Who did I think I was punishing?

Hanna: Same person you're punishing now.

Tom: I don't understand the first fucking thing about anything.

Hanna: For the same dumb lovely reason.

Tom: That's a fact.

Hanna: Stop it.

Tom: That's a natural fucking fact.

Hanna: *Stop* it.

Tom: I want my son. (*Beat*) I want my son back.

Pause.

Hanna: You can't have him, Tom.

Tom: I want to take him in my arms one more time and kiss him and hold him.

I want my son.

He breaks into tears and beats the cart violently with a clenched fist.

My son, my son, my beautiful son.

My beautiful son.

Pause. Hanna moves over to him. She puts her hands on his shoulders.

Hanna: You're killing yourself here. Come on, get up. Get up.

She pulls him to his feet. He tries to hide his face from her under the guise of wiping his eyes. She pulls out a Kleenex and wipes his face with it. He resists.

Get over here. Men. Christ.

Tom: Thank you.

Hanna: You're welcome. (*Pause*) What was your son's name?

Tom: Eddie. His name was Eddie. (*Beat*) If I let him go, then he's gone, right?

Hanna: Tom—

Tom: Then he's really gone?

Beat.

Hanna: I don't think I would've recognised Al's body if the nurse hadn't shown me. I could hardly bear to touch what was left at first. But I took his hand and I held it, and after a time his hand seemed to warm up, seemed to become so warm that just for a moment, I forgot. And I turned to look at his face, and I was so disappointed. I was so crushed by disappointment I could hardly breathe. (*Pause*) He's gone, Tom. He's really gone.

Pause.

Tom: Tell me some more about him. Your husband.

Hanna: I don't think so.

Tom: I knew some good Als.

Hanna: (*small smile*) Did you?

Tom: It'd be good for me to hear about him, I think.

Hanna: No.

Tom: Is it because—

Hanna: It's nothing personal. I don't tell anyone. People had their chance to hear the story before, and not one of them would hear it. They all had their agendas and their reasons and not one of them would simply listen. Everybody wanted to have their say and nobody wanted to listen. So it's mine now. I'm keeping him. It's what I have left.

Pause.

Tom: He wanted to know stuff, you know? He wanted to know everything. Made me feel old and sluggish, stupefied. And scared. Like he could see questions I woulda never even thought to ask. And then he had the drive to push on and keep asking them. *He wanted to know the answers.* I never in my life before the last two years wanted to know the answers. (*Beat*) I resented that. That he had that confidence, that willingness to go forward into the dark, these things his mother gave him...I was proud of him and I resented him. (*Beat. Quietly*) Do you think that's maybe why...?

Hanna: No. Of course not.

Tom: But you shouldn't...a father shouldn't...his own son—

Hanna: It was nothing to do with you.

Pause.

Tom: Where you gonna go after this?

Hanna: I don't know. I want to breathe. And I want to sing. I'm gonna keep trying for both those things. (*Beat*) You?

Tom: I...I'm not sure.

Hanna: What about your wife?

Tom: I don't have a wife no more.

Hanna: But you have a ring.

Beat.

Tom: Yeah.

Hanna: Go see your wife, Tom.

Blackout.

Scene Two

Tom and Ray at a Paterson bowling alley.

Ray: Shit is different now. (*Beat*) Take your shot.

Tom: What is that supposed to mean?

Ray: Take your spare, Tommy. (*Beat*). Tom takes his shot. He misses) You ain't been practising your bowling anyway, I'll tell you that.

Tom: Whaddya mean, shit is different?

Ray: You know I don't like distractions when it's my shot.

Tom: Ray—

Ray: I need to concentrate. (*Ray gestures to his ball. Beat. Tom gestures at him to get on with it*) Thank you. (*Beat. Ray takes his shot*) Rack 'em, baby! Still got the touch.

Tom: Tell me, Ray.

Ray: You don't beat around the fucking bush, do ya?! Sixteen months: not a call, a letter, an email—

Tom: You don't have email.

Ray: Sixteen months, Tommy! And not like we parted on the fucking best of terms exactly!

Tom: I know.

Ray: And now you're back and it's 'Hey Ray' and a coupla beers and a night at the alley is gonna wash it away? You ripped something out of me, Tommy. It takes a long fucking time to grow something and then someone can just chop it down overnight and you got nothing. You get no credit for the thing you used to have, none at all.

Tom: I know that.

Ray: It's hard out here for me too, you know. It's hard out here for everybody, not just you. You took the easy option and you ran away.

Tom: The *easy*—?

Ray: I stuck by you through thick and thin and you never even left me a forwarding address.

Pause.

Tom: I can't do what you want me to do, Ray.

Ray: I don't want you to *do* anything, shithead. (*Beat*) What the fuck are you even *living* on?

Tom: Pension.

Ray: You're living on a fireman's pension? (*He reaches into his pocket, pulls out $10 and proffers it to Tom*) You better let me pay for the beers.

Tom: Don't be a dick. (*Beat*) Put it away, Ray.

Pause. Ray puts the money away.

Ray: I seen you on TV. Pulling that fucking tombstone.

Tom: Yeah?

Ray: The hell was that about?

Tom: How'd I look?

Ray: You looked OK. Compared to the faggots and lentil-eaters and feminists you were with, you came across pretty decent. (*Beat*) Some of what you said even made sense.

Beat.

Tom: How you been?

Ray: I been OK. Like I said, shit is different. It's not the same faces in the station house. Lotta the guys moved to the city, fill the gaps. We got all kinds of people coming in from upstate…Not the same faces in the cab, y'know? Lotta changes. (*Beat*) Half the fuckin fire service is writing a *book*. I shit you not. I been asked do I know any good agents. Somebody told me, in the city, they got fire guys *body waxing*. Like an epidemic up there, they say. (*Beat*) Jimmy T's son, you remember little Sean? He signed up for Iraq. (*Beat*) He's back. His left foot ain't.

Beat.

Tom: How's Sophia doing?

Ray: She's good. She switched art classes, now she's bringing home *sculpture*. Is it a pig, is it a rabbit? *I* don't know. 'It's great, honey.' (*Beat*) Where did it go, Tom?

Tom: Where did what go?

Ray: The togetherness, you know, the solidarity. The things we was all gonna do together, for all of us.

Tom: I never felt that. I never got none of that.

Ray: It's just all back to me myself and I.

Pause.

Tom: I'm sorry, Ray.

Pause.

Ray: Susan's seeing someone else.

Tom: What?!

Ray: Dick.

Tom: Who the fuck is Dick?

Ray: What did you expect? You don't call, you don't write—

Tom: How long you known about this?

Ray: What did you think, she was just gonna wait for you?

Tom: You knew about this and you never let me know?

Ray: You didn't leave a forwarding address, Tommy.

Tom: She's my fucking wife.

Ray: Yeah? She's seeing someone else.

Scene Three

The Macfarlane living room. Tom with coat in one hand and package in the other.

Susan: He's my art teacher.

Pause.

Tom: He comes in here?

Susan: Yes, he comes in here.

Tom: You fuck him here, in my house?

Susan: It's my house, Tom. I live here.

Tom: You fuck him here?

Susan: Yes. I do.

Pause.

Tom: Brought you something.

He hands her the package.

Susan: You don't have to—

Tom: What I am gonna do, take it back now? I lost the receipt. Open it. (*Beat. She opens it. It's a beautiful box of art supplies. She looks at it. Pause. He indicates his coat*) I looked for the thing, the hang up thing—

Susan: The *hook*?

Tom: It moved. You moved the thing.

Susan: Give it to me.

She leaves and returns without the coat and box. Pause.

Tom: Art teacher, huh? That's good. Somebody 'cultured'.

Susan: Don't.

Tom: All the things I could never give you.

Beat.

Susan: (*exasperated*) Yeah, well, you gave me an awful lot else, so—

Tom: It's 'gave' now?!

Susan: Sixteen months!

Tom: Jesus fucking Christ.

Susan: Yes, it's 'gave' when you haven't seen someone for—

Tom: It's 'gave' now? Fuck me.

Susan: Since you put it that way, yes: fuck you, Thomas. Did you seriously think you could just waltz back in here and dinner would be on the table? 'Hi honey, I'm home!' 'How was your day, dear?' 'It was great—I towed this huge rock around the eastern seaboard and now everybody associates my kid with the anti-war movement.'

Tom: I didn't—

Susan: I guess you won, didn't you? Congratulations.

Tom: Won what?

Susan: Our little tug of war.

Tom: I didn't win nothing, believe me.

Susan: You took Eddie.

Tom: I did not.

Susan: You got to decide who he was.

Tom: I didn't take him, they took him.

Susan: They took him and then you took him.

Tom: I don't have him, Susan.

Susan: Well, I don't have him either.

Pause. Tom looks around.

Twom: I been here so much in my head it's like what's in my head is the real thing and this is the imagination, you know? (*Beat*) How've you been, Susie?

Beat.

Susan: Shitty. Shitty, Tom. Thanks for asking.

Tom: How's school?

Susan: School sucks, actually. I don't care any more.

Tom: I doubt that.

Susan: I don't care any more. I don't care about the wellbeing of other people's children.

Beat.

Tom: That's a shame. You were always a great teacher.

Susan: I hear him crying. I hear him crying in this house as plainly as I hear you, I swear it. I hear him crying as a young child and it terrifies me. I'm not making it up.

Tom: I believe you.

Susan: I'm not that kind, you know that.

Tom: We never lived in this house when Eddie was young.

Susan: I know that. But that is what I hear. (*Beat*) You're the only person who didn't take a half step back when I told them that. (*Beat*) I feel like such a failure. I feel like such a complete and utter worthless failure. (*She is on the edge of tears. He steps forward instinctively*) Please don't…Please. (*Beat. He steps back*) Everything I ever wanted to achieve, it's gone. My university career, I met you, I let that go.

Tom: (*wincing*) I shoulda—

Susan: I let that go, that's on me. My marriage. My son.

Tom: You didn't—

Susan: (*real anger*) Why didn't you let me finish my memorial, Tommy? Do you not realise who that was for? It was for you and me and Eddie, all three of us. It was for you, you stupid…It was my apology to you! For taking him away from you.

Tom: You didn't take him away from me.

Susan: Not in my mind, but in yours I did. Because he was yours when he was young and mine when he got older and I know how much that hurt you, even though it was his choice. I painted him the way you'd always wanted him to be, the way you always *told* me you wanted him to be anyway, and it seemed like it was the way everybody else wanted him to be too, and that felt good to me, it felt good that everybody wanted that and loved me for it and I could give it to them. (*Beat*) If you'd kept your mouth shut for two minutes, we could've seen how much he was loved. You ruined our chance to see how much everybody loved him. Why'd you have to do that, Tom?

Tom: I wanted it to be the truth.

Susan: It was the truth! Everybody was there.

Tom: Including those assholes.

Susan: Forget them! Forget the politics.

Tom: When the politics never forget us? I can't forget 'em.

Susan: But you could forget me.

Tom: I wanted it to be the truth. We were all so scared we couldn't stand that?

Susan: That was our chance to see how Eddie was loved, and it won't come back.

Tom: Because they stole it from us.

Susan: When something's gone, does it matter how?

Tom: It matters.

Susan: It matters that it's gone. (*Pause*) People don't come round any more, I suppose you know that? I had a terrible row with Sophia as soon as I stopped being the grateful victim.

Tom: I could never understand…I mean, you and her always hated each other until…

Susan: I wanted to be loved, Tom. I wanted to be loved and she seemed to want to…

Beat.

Tom: Once, when he was little, he fell down and he was screaming like something out of a war movie, and I picked him up and held him and I dared God to give me all his pain, always, because I had a secret reservoir of strength for him that nobody and nothing could ever drain and I knew that, I knew that like nothing I've ever known. (*Beat*) What do I do with that reservoir now? *Why didn't God take the dare?* (*Pause*) Why wouldn't he be a fireman, Susie? Why wouldn't he?

Susan: Because he didn't want to, Tom. (*Beat*) Everything feels temporary and unreal, like any moment the bubble will pop and you and Eddie will come back through the door and everything can go back to normal. And at the same time it feels like things have always been this way, like I've never had a say in anything, like it was all mapped out. At least when you were bull-headed and cruel and arrogant, you were making your own decisions. I feel like I've been reading from a script, lines someone forced into my hand, from the very first day. (*Beat*) That was a compliment. You might've missed it cos it was hidden under the bull-headed arrogant stuff, but scrape that aside and there's a compliment under there.

Tom: The thing I regret most is that I wasn't able to take the weight off you.

Susan: And I you, Tom.

Tom: Because I thought, and I still think, that the truth is what will take that weight away. (*She shrugs*) I want us again.

Susan: No.

Tom: Why not?

Susan: Because what are we now? After all this? What would we be? Something always dwelling in the past, always dragged under by something black and rotten?

Beat.

Tom: I don't know.

Susan: There are some things once done that can't be undone. There's some things that can't survive being dragged out into the light.

Tom: But I'm willing to try.

Susan: We crossed a line, or we were pulled across it, and it's not our fault but I don't think we can go back.

Tom: I want to try.

Susan: It's too late, Tom. A live marriage can't compete with a dead child.

Pause.

Tom: I would like to make you change your mind. (*Beat*) Will you give me the chance to change your mind?

Susan: I'm seeing someone.

Tom: Fuck your art teacher.

Susan: Very persuasive, Tommy. Very refined.

Tom: I don't know what else to say. Words have betrayed me a lot. Please.

Susan: I don't know. I don't think so.

Tom: Please. (*Beat*) Think about it?

Pause.

Susan: Let me get us a drink.

Tom: I could use one, sure.

Susan: Me too.

They stand still. Pause. Lights gradually down.

HIGHCLIFFE CASTLE

GW00598371

AND

THE CLARETIANS

1953-1966

HARRY SALSBURY

British Library Cataloguing-in-Publication data. A catalogue
for this book is available from the British Library.

Published by Natula Publications
              5 St Margaret's Avenue
              Christchurch BH23 1JD.

              www.natula.co.uk

Front Cover illustration: Claretians outside South Porch,
Highcliffe Castle, 1960.

Back Cover illustration: Students & Faculty, 1957.

Illustrations on pages: 12,28,31,32,34,36,66 and Back Cover
Courtesy of Walter Müller's archive.

Illustrations on pages: 19,26,37,46,49,55,59 and 61
Courtesy of Ian Stevenson's collection.

Other illustrations are the author's own.

"Seek out ye goode in everie man,
And speke of all the best ye can."

Geoffrey Chaucer

**To the Memory of
The Reverend Stephen Emaldia C.M.F.,
who brought the Claretians to Highcliffe Castle**

and

**The Reverend Arthur S. Crook C.M.F.,
its first Father Superior
and Novice Master
also some time College Rector
who loved the place.**

ACKNOWLEDGEMENTS

My thanks to my dear wife, Margaret, for spending many hours word processing, checking and correcting the script and offering excellent advice.

My sincere thanks also to Walter Müller of Stuttgart in Germany, a former student of the College at Highcliffe Castle for his kind loan of invaluable archive material. He is an expert on Highcliffe Castle, which he still loves and visits.

Finally to Michael Allen, the first Manager of the restored Highcliffe Castle for suggesting and supporting this brochure and his provision of some copies of *The Claretian* of 1964.

ABOUT THE AUTHOR

The Reverend Harry Salsbury entered the Claretian Congregation at Highcliffe Castle in August 1954. He was ordained in the Claretian Parish Church at Hayes in July 1961. He married in 1980 and became Assistant Master and Chaplain at Brighton College Preparatory School, where he taught Divinity, Latin and English until retiring in 1993.

He lives with his wife Margaret in Eastbourne, East Sussex. They have four children and one grandchild. He is the author of *Highcliffe Castle, a History and Guide*, first published in 1960.

CONTENTS

ILLUSTRATIONS

Page No.

INTRODUCTION
WHO WERE THE CLARETIANS?

The 'Claretians' who occupied Highcliffe Castle from 1953 to 1966 had for their official title the 'Congregation Of The Missionary Sons Of The Immaculate Heart of Mary', and the letters C.M.F. which each Claretian put after his name stood for 'Cordis Mariae Filius, Son of the Heart of Mary'.

They were founded in 1849, in Spain, by St. Anthony Claret who later became Archbishop of Santiago Cuba and then Royal Confessor to Queen Isabella II of Spain. The 19th century had seen a great flowering in church missionary activity and a number of Missionary Congregations were founded at that time, each with a title related to the Blessed Virgin Mary. They became known as the 'Marian Congregations'. The Claretians were one of these.

In time, popular usage accorded them the name 'Claretian' after their founder St. Anthony Claret, and this is how they are usually known. In this case the letters C.M.F. after their name means 'Claretian Missionary Father' although there are many Claretian lay brothers who are not priests.

Strictly speaking the Claretians are not a religious order but a religious congregation. The difference is that members of a religious order live in a monastery, wear a distinctive religious habit with a cowl and make solemn vows. They are known as monks. They follow a life of prayer and meditation and engage in manual work so as to render their monastery self-sufficient.

Monks are bound to remain within their monastery and do not go outside it except with permission and for a very serious reason. The head of the monastery is the Abbot who is elected for life by the other monks. Each monastery is completely independent of all

7

St. Anthony Claret, 1807-1870
Founder of the Claretian Missionaries

other monasteries of the same order. When a man wishes to become a monk he seeks admission to the monastery of his choice. If he is accepted and comes to make his monastic vows he will remain there all his life.

Members of a Religious Congregation live in community in a religious house and make simple vows. They are known as religious. They are not monks and they do not live in a monastery. They can expect to live in several different religious houses during their lifetime.

Each religious house has a Father Superior as its head who is usually appointed for three years. A group of religious houses forms a province. The head of a province is the Father Provincial who holds office usually for six years. Provinces are found in different countries throughout the world. The overall head of all the provinces is the Superior General who is based in Rome. He is assisted by a group of advisers called General Consulters.

Members of a religious congregation do not wear a distinctive religious habit with a cowl, as do the monastic orders. Their usual dress is the clerical cassock with perhaps some distinguishing mark appended. The Claretians wear a black cassock and sash no different to any other priest although it nevertheless has the status of a religious habit.

Anyone wishing to join a Religious Congregation would have to be approved by the Father Provincial. He would have to spend a period in the Congregation, not wearing the habit, to clarify in his own mind the correctness of his choice. This is known as the postulancy and its minimum length is two weeks. The applicant is known as a postulant.

The postulant then spends one year as a novice in the noviciate learning the Claretian way of life. He then takes simple vows of poverty, chastity and obedience for one year and begins his studies for the priesthood which lasts for six years. During this time he renews his vows annually until after three years he makes his final vows for life. After six years study the student is ordained priest and appointed to work as a priest at one of the religious houses in the province.

Highcliffe Castle was a Religious House serving first as a Noviciate, 1953-1956, and then as a College or Seminary, 1956-1966 within the Anglo Irish Province. It was here that Claretian students studied for the priesthood.

DISCOVERY

In 1953, three senior members of the Claretian Congregation came to Highcliffe. They were Father Stephen Emaldia, Head of the Claretians in England, his deputy, Father Arthur Crook and Father Lucian Olivares, acting as an advisor. They had come to survey a mansion property with a view to purchasing it for the Congregation's use. It was then that the Fathers were told about Highcliffe Castle and its availability. At once they went to have a look at it.

At that time Highcliffe Castle was approached along the drive from the entrance lodges on the Lymington Road through the surrounding park to the impressive North Portico. The Claretian Fathers made their way along the drive and had their first view of Highcliffe Castle. They were overwhelmed by what they had discovered. They believed at once that Highcliffe Castle was ideal for the purpose they had in mind of its becoming a college for Claretian students studying to become priests. They all felt that God was blessing the Congregation in England by leading them to this magnificent building and arrangements speedily went ahead for its purchase.

THE CLARETIANS IN ENGLAND

The Claretian Congregation was not numerous or widespread in England in 1953. They administered two parishes, one at Hayes in Middlesex, the other at Loughton in Essex. They had come to Hayes in 1912 acquiring a beautiful property, Botwell House and its grounds, and in 1927 established a parish at Loughton, since relinquished. There would have been about eight Claretian Fathers and two lay Brothers to administer these two parishes. All were Spanish save for Father Crook, the only English member in the Congregation who had joined after the First World War and was ordained in 1928. He was later sent to the United States where he became a Parish Priest and Father Superior.

The Claretians made no effort to expand beyond their two parishes in England, but in the early 1950's the Superior General of the Congregation and his advisers in Rome decided to change all that. They wanted the Congregation to increase in England and to expand into Ireland. It was said that the Superior General was ambitious for personnel from England and Ireland to establish the Congregation in the Commonwealth, Australia, and New Zealand being envisaged.

To set all this in motion a Claretian Father noted for his drive, administrative ability and a deep spirituality was put in charge in England. This was Father Stephen Emaldia, who had served for many years in America where his achievements had caught the attention of the Claretian Superiors in Rome.

It seems likely that Father Crook's recall to England at that time was part of the plan to increase and expand the Congregation in England. He was, after all, the only English priest in the entire Congregation which had some 4,000 members worldwide.

Students and Faculty 1958

Centre front: Fr. Peter Schweiger C.M.F. Superior General on a visit from Rome.
On his right: Fr. Stephen Emaldia, Provincial Superior.

12

NOVICIATE   1953

All Religious Orders and Congregations had a year of preliminary training in which its new members learned about the way of life membership entailed. This was not a year of academic study. It was a spiritual year when the new members learned the art and technique of prayer and meditation, and became accustomed to living in a religious community.

This spiritual year was called the Noviciate Year, the religious house in which it was followed was called the Noviciate House, the new members were known as Novices and the priest responsible for their training was the Novice Master. It was decided that Highcliffe Castle should become the Noviciate House with Father Crook as Novice Master and Father Superior.

And so in August 1953 Father Crook took over at Highcliffe Castle as the first Novice Master. He had just three Novices. It was customary for the Claretian Noviciate Year to begin on 21st August, the day before the Congregation's titular Feast of the Immaculate Heart of Mary. It was preceded by a period of ten days taken up with prayer, spiritual talks and meditation. These ten days were known as a spiritual retreat and were a preparation before starting the Noviciate.

Then at an impressive ceremony in the Drawing Room Chapel the Novices received the religious habit. This was known as the clothing ceremony at which the Novices were 'clothed' in the Claretian habit that was a black clerical cassock and sash. The Head of the Congregation in England presided at this first clothing ceremony in Highcliffe Castle.   That was Father Emaldia. The Novices had now 'entered' the Congregation. Two more Novices were clothed on 22nd October, on the day preceding the Feast of St. Anthony Claret, Founder of the Claretian Missionaries.

PROGRESS

As part of the scheme of expansion in England some students were transferred from other countries. They came from the United States and Germany where they had completed their Noviciate Year. An English and an Irish student who had made their Noviciate in Spain were with them. The English student subsequently went to Rome to complete his studies.

As there was no Claretian College in England these young men attended Oscott College, near Birmingham. They lived in a large house in Streetly, Staffordshire near Oscott College, purchased by the Congregation to serve as a House of Studies. Two of these students from the 1950's are still with the Claretians in England.

The new policy of expansion began to yield fruit. On 21st August 1954, Father Emaldia clothed seven Novices in the Drawing Room Chapel and on 22nd October, two more. Of these nine, three were English and six were Irish. Five eventually became priests of whom one was still serving as a Claretian at the turn of the century. On the day after, 22nd August, the Feast of the Immaculate Heart of Mary, two Novices who had persevered from the previous year made their first religious vows during Mass in the Drawing Room Chapel. These vows were to obey the holy Constitutions of the Claretian Congregation: Obedience; to eschew the possession of money and property, Poverty; and to remain unmarried and celibate, Chastity. These vows were binding for one year and would be renewed for a second year and again for a third. At the end of three years in vows the candidate made his final vows that were binding for life.

THE LIFE OF A NOVICE AT HIGHCLIFFE

Joining or entering a Religious Order or Congregation was rather like going into the Army. I had been a National Service soldier and knew how you had to learn about a soldier's life and the Army's way of doing things. To be a good soldier you had to be trained - licked into shape and you led a life of strict discipline. Entering the Claretians was much the same. You underwent training; you were licked into shape and led a life of strict discipline. The Noviciate Year was the equivalent of a new recruits period of basic training in the Army.

The Novice's day began with a six o'clock morning call and he was expected to rise promptly. Chapel at 6.30 a.m. began with Morning Prayer followed by meditation until Mass began at 7.15 a.m. In those days the Mass was said in Latin and the priest stood with his back to the people. After Mass each made his own silent thanksgiving and at 8.00 a.m. it was time to make beds and wash hands before breakfast. This frugal meal, of porridge, bread and marmalade, like all meals, was eaten in silence as we listened to a fellow novice reading aloud from a spiritual book. The meal over, all went to the chapel to recite or pray the Morning Office.

In the monastic orders praying the Divine Office is, after the Mass the most important function of the day. It has been called the 'Magnum Opus' the great work and the 'Opus Dei', the work of God. The Divine Office is a form of prayer based on the Psalms and Scripture readings which is spread across the whole day, and in some Orders, the night as well. In those long past Latin, pre-Vatican Council days the office was divided by hours into Prime (First Hour), Terce (Third Hour), Sext (Sixth Hour) and None (Ninth Hour). The office hours were reckoned according to the Biblical Jewish way of counting time whereby the first hour of the day began at 6.00 a.m. So Prime was said at

6.00 a.m., Terce at 9.00 a.m., Sext at noon and None at 3.00 p.m. The principal offices were Matins (morning) and Lauds (praises) which were said before Prime at a very early hour - in some Orders this was at 2.00 a.m. Vespers were evening prayers said around 6.00 p.m. and Compline was the final office of the day. The monastic orders sang the Divine Office in a special form of music called plainsong and attended chapel seven times in the day to do so. The beauty, simplicity and purity of the Divine Office being sung by monks in plainsong can truly move and uplift the spirit.

The Claretian Novices, however, did not use the long Roman Office. They recited what was known as 'the Little Office of the Blessed Virgin Mary', which is a much shorter and simpler version. Prime, Terce, Sext and None were all said consecutively after breakfast. Matins and Lauds were said later in the day and Vespers and Compline were said in the early evening before supper.

After saying the Little Office in Chapel immediately following breakfast, the Novices went to their study room that was situated in the Conservatory at the fireplace end. During the cold winter months the Novices used the Library for their study room. At nine o'clock the Novice Master came to give an instruction about the religious life, or prayer and meditation or a lesson about the history of the Claretian Congregation and the life of its founder, St. Anthony Claret. Father Crook was an excellent and erudite speaker who held his listeners' attention and interest by his rich treasury of personal anecdote based on his own long and eventful life as a priest.

After this instruction there was half an hour of free time called 'recreation'. This was customarily spent by the Novices walking in groups with the Novice Master, around the paths or across the meadow and down the steps for a quick turn on the beach. The rest of the morning was given to housework and general manual work. In a building as large as the Castle with its extensive gardens there was plenty to be done each day. After work time there were noon prayers in the Chapel from the Claretian manual of prayers accompanied by Bible reading from the Old and New Testaments. Then came lunch followed by another opportunity to perambulate. A quiet period for private prayer or spiritual reading followed. Then there was office to pray in Chapel and the Rosary was said.

Although there was ostensibly no academic study in the Noviciate it was considered appropriate that the Novices should keep fresh their knowledge of Latin. So there was a Latin revision lesson each afternoon. Tea and afternoon recreation gave an hour's free time when a favourite pursuit was football on a piece of rough land at the front of the Castle, west of the Great Portico, since built upon. A turn on the beach was also favoured and in bad weather, billiards on a small table in the library was popular.

Occasionally whole days were given to manual work when there were special tasks to be done such as sweeping up leaves and tidying the gardens at the onset of Autumn. On one memorable occasion Father Crook led the Novices on a day excursion to the Isle of Wight where Quarr Abbey was visited. They also took in Beaulieu and Bucklers Hard. Apart from this outing, the Novices were confined to the Castle except on Thursdays when they had their walk afternoon. Laying aside their black cassocks and dressed in mufti they set off in an animated group making their way towards Christchurch, New Milton, Hinton Admiral or along the beach to Mudeford or Barton-on-Sea.

THE HOLY CONSTITUTIONS

All Religious Orders have a Holy Rule that sets out the precepts and instructions according to which their members are expected to conduct and shape their lives.

The Claretian Congregation had their 'Holy Constitutions' drawn up at its foundation by St. Anthony Claret and developed by its first Father members. In addition to this there was a book of additional laws, formulated in later years, which supplemented the Holy Constitutions. These two regulatory volumes seemed to comprehensively cover every aspect of life in the Congregation. There was a rule that forbade smoking and the taking of snuff and another that banned the eating of chicken. Poultry was expensive in those pre-broiler house days and it was considered inappropriate for Claretians who had taken a vow of poverty to spend large sums on chicken and cigarettes. Curiously, alcoholic drinks which would have been equally or even more costly were not proscribed. The Holy constitutions were intended to be the keystone of every Claretian's life. A good Claretian was one who obeyed all the Holy Constitutions and its supplementary additional laws to the letter. A good Claretian was an observant Claretian.

CELEBRATIONS

There were times for celebrations, to relax a little from the daily routine and to lighten up. These were on the greater religious Festivals and Christmas and Easter were truly happy occasions.

A great celebratory day was the Feast of St. Anthony Claret on 23rd October, (since moved to 24th October), when all the Claretians commemorate their Holy Founder. Also given great prominence was the Novice Master's birthday, known as his

'Feast Day', when visitors came from the communities in Hayes and Loughton to join in the celebrations.

The biggest celebration of all was Profession Day when the Novices made their First Vows of Poverty, Chastity and Obedience at the end of their Noviciate Year. This customarily took place on the Feast of the Immaculate Heart of Mary on 22nd August, the Titular Feast of the Claretian Congregation whose each member styled himself, Cordis Mariae Filius, Son of the Heart of Mary.

Baroque Angel Baptismal Font situated atop Bute Sundial used as garden ornament.

What a day that was for the Novices who had been preparing themselves for it spiritually for the whole year. Ten days before the great day silence fell on the Noviciate House as the Novices began their final concerted preparation for making their Religious Profession of Vows. This was the spiritual retreat devoted to prayer and meditation conducted by the Novice Master who gave two spiritual talks in the Chapel each day for the guidance and inspiration of the Novices. All this was in an atmosphere of silent recollection. There were no recreation times, no light conversation; people only spoke when absolutely necessary.

But novices are young, they were the Benjamins of the Claretian family, and it was Father Crook's wont to 'raise silence' at tea-time on occasions. This lightening up helped everybody. Father Crook was the consummate Retreat Master with a wide reputation for his spirituality and he was in great demand from other Religious Institutes to conduct Retreats. His spiritual talks helped every body and he had the great gift of making people laugh - he was a very humorous man.

Then Profession Day arrived. The Claretians were a family that recognised and valued the wider family of its members' relatives. So mums and dads, brothers and sisters, uncles and aunts and grandparents too came flocking to the Noviciate House to witness their young relative make his Religious Profession. How proud and happy they all felt, although perhaps a little tearful too.

The atmosphere of the Profession Mass was one of joy and happiness and for those professing their vows it was a profound religious experience in which everyone who was present shared.

Each Novice knelt before the Father Provincial to make his vows that were spoken in Latin. As soon as the Novices had made their vows all the other Claretians who were there flocked into the Sanctuary to join the Father Provincial and Novice Master in giving each newly professed member of the Congregation the traditional bear-hug of welcome into the Claretian family. From then on it was fun and laughter all the way. A splendid alfresco lunch with proud parents, loving brothers and sisters, doting aunts and uncles, fond grandparents too all enjoying a marvellous family day out with a difference.

Stern years of study and spiritual formation lay ahead of these idealistic young men but they set off into them from their Noviciate Profession Day with hearts full of joy and determination. The responsibility of the Fathers given the onerous task of guiding and helping those young men through those years was awesome. Only priests of the highest spiritual, intellectual and personal calibre were considered for the demanding role of educating, forming, guiding and inspiring these young candidates for the priesthood.

And what about all those close relatives who had been present on Profession Day? It was the Claretian's custom to welcome and encourage close relatives and friends to visit the students at the College during holiday times. Many did so and although there was no guest accommodation in the College itself, friends and neighbours of the Claretians were very pleased and happy to take in parents who had come to visit. The warm and familiar contact between the students' relatives, the College and the Claretian Congregation as a whole was an attractive feature of the Claretian life and ethos.

This contact was further enhanced by the introduction of parents' weeks in August when mums and dads who attended their sons' renewal of vows in the College Chapel at Highcliffe on the 22nd August, Feast of the Immaculate of Mary, were invited to stay on for a few days. A good number of parents and relatives accepted this generous Claretian hospitality and everyone enjoyed a very happy family week.

Profession Day, August 1958. Student and relatives.

THE SCHOOL

The Claretians also established a small school for boys at Highcliffe Castle in 1954. These boys all intended to join the Congregation as novices when they were old enough to do so. Such a school was known as a junior seminary. At Highcliffe it occupied the Penleaze Wing and had its own chapel situated in the former dining room. These schoolboys or junior seminarians were also known as 'Postulants', the official name for anyone intending to enter a Religious Order or Congregation and living in one of its religious houses.

There was no fraternisation between Novices and Postulants as the Holy Constitutions decreed that Novices should have no contact with other members of the community or with visitors. They had to be sheltered from all outside influences and distractions while they followed the strict life of their formative year. The school at Highcliffe eventually moved to a splendid complex of buildings ideally suited for use as a school at Buckden in Huntingdonshire. This was a former Palace of the Bishops of Lincoln that after passing into private hands had come to the Roman Catholic Diocese of Northampton. The Bishop of Northampton, under an agreement with the Claretians, offered it to them for their own purpose that was to be as a school or junior seminary.

THE LAST NOVICIATE AT HIGHCLIFFE
1955-1956

The third and last noviciate at Highcliffe Castle, 1955-56 was a good indication of the Congregation's remarkable growth and progress in England. On the 21st August 1955, fifteen Novices were clothed in the Drawing Room Chapel. On the day following the seven Novices who had completed their Noviciate year made their first vows and a few days later made their way to the House of Studies at Streetly. These seven were not to attend Oscott College as Streetly was now a mini-college for eleven students with a faculty of four priests to provide lectures. The Oscott-attending students were now all ordained priests save for two who continued to cycle over from Streetly to attend lectures. But a year later in 1956 the College or Seminary was established at Highcliffe Castle. The Claretians had acquired a beautiful mansion, Backwell Hill House near Bristol, to which the Noviciate had been duly transferred. Previously, Backwell Hill House had been owned by the Wills family of 'Woodbine' and 'Gold Flake' fame.

The Claretian Congregation seemed to have had a talent for acquiring imposing buildings for its various needs. They had purchased Highcliffe Castle for their College, then Backwell Hill House for their Noviciate and finally Buckden Palace became theirs for use as a school. It was an impressive list of acquired real estate.

THE COLLEGE AT HIGHCLIFFE, 1956

So in the summer of 1956 Highcliffe Castle became the college for Claretian students in England studying for the priesthood. In the Roman Catholic Church such a college is usually known as a Seminary, while retaining its title, and the students are known as seminarians. The usage at Highcliffe was to speak of the College and its students. The terms seminary and seminarians were not favoured, at least for official purposes.

At the time of the establishment of the college at Highcliffe Castle in 1956 the future of the Claretian Congregation in England seemed assured. The School or Postulancy, the Noviciate and the College were all flourishing and there was no lack of new recruits. The ranks at Highcliffe were further increased by the arrival of several students from Germany, Austria and Portugal. A friendly football match played one afternoon between teams of priests and students had nine different nationalities among the twenty-two players. The College certainly had an international flavour although there was a strict rule that English be spoken at all times.

<u>COLLEGE ROUTINE</u>

The student's life was a very strict one. The Holy Constitutions were followed to the letter along with its book of additional rules. And if they were not enough there was another book of rules drawn up for the particular governance of colleges with their faculties and students. They made a formidable trilogy and Rectors and Prefects who were the student's directors had a tendency to wax on rather about rule keeping. Needless to say, the students were on the whole a pretty respectable and blameless bunch.

The rising hour was half past five with morning prayers, meditation, Mass and thanksgiving in Chapel going on until half past seven when there was an hour of study before breakfast. All the lectures were in the morning with a half an hour recreation break at 10 a.m. There were noon prayers in the Chapel followed by lunch and a recreation break from half past twelve to half past one. There were more prayers in Chapel at two but the students did not say the Little Office as did the Novices. Then it was teatime at four and free time until five. After this there were other activities as well as studies, spaced out through the week, as elocution lessons, discussion groups, choir practice, music and drama. Supper was at seven followed by free time. Night prayers were at nine and included a spiritual talk from the Father Rector or one of the faculty.

Highcliffe Castle, Claretian Major Seminary

WHAT THEY STUDIED

Candidates for the Roman Catholic Priesthood followed a course of studies lasting six years. The first two years were spent in the study of philosophy while the next four were devoted to theology and allied subjects. The faculty comprised of Claretian priests who were all well qualified in their subjects. They were of various nationalities, Spanish, Spanish-Basque, German, Argentinean, Mexican, American, Chinese and English.

The philosophy students studied Scholastic Philosophy based on the philosophical works of the great thirteenth century scholar, St. Thomas Aquinas that stemmed from the ancient Greek philosopher, Aristotle of the 3rd century B.C. The textbook for the course was written by a learned Benedictine monk who was a professor at the Gregorian University in Rome. A grainy frontispiece photograph of his unsmiling, bespectacled face looking away from the camera neither flattered him nor encouraged the readers of his learned, but now dated, work. The four years course in Theology consisted in the study of dogmatic Theology and moral Theology. The first was concerned with all aspects of Christian doctrine and was based on the works of St. Thomas Aquinas, the second dealt with Christian moral precepts and their application.

The Philosophy and Theology textbooks were all in Latin. The paramount importance of Latin had been recently re-emphasised by the Vatican and its use as the language for philosophy and theology text books was regarded as a sure means of avoiding erroneous thinking in those subjects. In the Roman Catholic Church it was held that Latin terms were capable of only one meaning and understanding whereas the many national languages in daily colloquial use had too many shades of meaning and could easily lead to error. It was an interesting point of view and the students at Highcliffe were fortunate to have their lectures in

English and not Latin.

For their Old and New Testament studies the students had textbooks in English but there were crash courses in Hebrew and New Testament Greek as the Bible had to be read and understood in its original languages rather than in translation. Church History, Church Law, Elocution and Music were included in the course.

HOLY ORDERS

The students at Highcliffe were all studying for the priesthood so understandably they all looked forward to the great day when they would be ordained priest.

**The author receiving the tonsure from
Archbishop-Bishop King, 1958**

28

In those days there were a number of stages to be passed through on the way to the priesthood and each stage was welcome by the student as a sign that Ordination Day was drawing ever nearer.

The first stage was to receive the clerical tonsure from the Bishop of the Diocese. In the past ages all priest and clerics had the crown of their head shaved. This was known as the tonsure and indicated that the person was a cleric. Monks in their monasteries had the entire top of the head shaved when they received the religious habit. The tonsure was looked upon as a sign of penance and dedication to God's service. Students received the tonsure during the second year of their theology course. At a simple evening service the Bishop snipped a small token amount of hair from the crown of the student's head saying the appropriate prayer. This made the student officially a member of the clergy for he was now a tonsured cleric.

The next morning after receiving the tonsure the student received the first two minor orders from the Bishop. These were the orders of Reader and Doorkeeper that empowered their recipient to read at church services and to have custody of the church keys.

During his third year of theology studies the student received the third and fourth minor orders of Acolyte and Exorcist from the Bishop. The order of Acolyte conferred the right to serve the priest at Mass but the order of Exorcist was not understood to give power to drive out evil spirits. Then at the beginning of his final year of study the student was ordained Subdeacon by the Bishop. The Subdeacon had only one function and that was to be a minor officiating minister at the Tridentine Solemn High Mass when he wore an Alb - a full-length white linen garment and a vestment called a Dalmatic. He also wore a strip of material on his left wrist called a Maniple. A Subdeacon was also obliged to say each day, but in private, the Roman Divine Office.

After the Second Vatican Council as part of the liturgical reforms all these Minor Orders were suppressed. This was because none of them had any scriptural foundation and they lacked any practical significance, and they were certainly not Sacraments. They were now recognised as simply ecclesiastical customs invented by the Church and devoid of any scriptural or theological meaning. Yes, they were accretions all right but countless generations of priest had felt encouraged and uplifted upon receiving these now defunct orders that gave them a great sense of identity as ordinands and future priests. It was certainly my own experience at the time.

Half way through his final year of six years of studies, the student was ordained Deacon by the Bishop. The Holy Order of Deacon has its origin in the New Testament of the Bible and is truly a Holy Sacrament. A Deacon had the power to administer the Sacrament of Baptism and Extreme Unction, since renamed the Sacrament of the Sick, to administer Holy Communion, to preach, to conduct weddings and to take funerals. He was also bound to say in private each day the Roman Divine Office.

Then at the end of his six years of studies came the great day when the student was at last ordained a Priest. As well as the powers he had received as a Deacon he could now celebrate Mass and hear Confessions. The Priesthood was a Sacrament instituted by Jesus at the Last Supper, and conferred by his representative, the Diocesan Bishop. The first Claretian priest to be ordained in the Great Hall Chapel at Highcliffe Castle was Father Kieran Vaughan.

It was customarily the Bishop of Portsmouth who carried out the Ordinations in the Great hall Chapel at Highcliffe. In the 1950's and early 1960's this was Archbishop-Bishop King. He was a venerable figure, much loved, deeply respected and widely popular throughout his Diocese and beyond. Pope Pius Xll conferred upon him the honorary rank of Archbishop, a true reflection of the enormous esteem in which Archbishop-Bishop King was everywhere held.

"Ecce Sacerdos magnus qui in diebus suis placuit Deo".

Newly ordained Claretian priests giving their first blessing to the ordaining Bishop of Portsmouth, 1959.

And what of Ordination Day itself? Who can describe what was the greatest day in a Claretian student's life? After all those long years of spiritual and academic preparation came the great day when the student became a priest. This above all other considerations was what had driven the student on through fair weather and foul, this was his final objective, his ultimate goal, for he had no other ambition or desire except to be a priest.

The welcome presence of the Bishop in the College was enough to create a benign and pleasant atmosphere all of its own. The ordinands had made their ten-day spiritual retreat in immediate preparation for their Ordination. Again, the wider family of students' relatives was there in great numbers as it had been at their sons' first religious profession those six years ago.

Students' ordination to Diaconate and Minor Orders, 1960

32

The Ordination Mass of those days was according to the old Tridentine Rite and entirely in Latin. The ceremony passed smoothly and magnificently with its ancient and holy ritual rich in the symbolism that accompanies the making of a new priest. It was a joyful and moving occasion for everyone for all believed profoundly in the Gospel and in the Church and its Holy Sacraments. It was an age of Faith, Conviction and Commitment when wide religious practice prevailed.

After the Ordination Mass the new priests gave their first priestly blessing starting with the Bishop himself who knelt humbly to be blessed by the new priests he had ordained and to kiss their consecrated hands. Then all came forward one by one for the first blessing, parents and all close relatives, Claretian fathers and students and brothers, friends and neighbours. It was a wonderful time, for "Haec Dies Quam Fecit Dominus, Exsultemus et Laetemur in Ea".

Then came the gaudeamus of the splendid Ordination Day lunch at which the Bishop presided. Ordinations were in July and the sun always seemed to shine on the outdoor meal. Everyone had a wonderful time; it was a great family occasion for everyone.

For the first time in their Claretian lives the new priest had an actual vacation with no strings attached. They were free to go home with their families and the next morning each would celebrate his first Mass, usually in his own Parish Church. A priest's first mass was also a great and memorable occasion and the attendance would be huge, for people loved to attend a new priest's first Mass and to receive his first blessing afterwards.

There was a celebratory breakfast and it is safe to say that celebrations would have filled the day and continued to the end of the new priest's holiday. Then it would be time to return to college and to receive his first appointment as a priest and to start his priestly work.

The last Ordinations to the priesthood and Diaconate to be held in the Great Hall College Chapel at Highcliffe Castle took place on 18th July 1965. On that historic occasion it was the Apostolic Delegate to Great Britain, Archbishop Cardinale, who ordained the two new priests. The Apostolic Delegate is the Pope's personal representative and a very important personage indeed having precedence over all the other Catholic Archbishops and Bishops in the Land. There can be no doubt that all the Claretians felt honoured by his presence among them.

Apostolic Delegate, Archbishop Cardinale
with two newly ordained Claretian priests and deacon.

34

THE COLLEGE CHAPEL

With the establishment of a college with a large student body and faculty it was necessary to have a chapel of adequate size. The Novitiate Chapel had been in the drawing room but that was now considered too small. It was decided that the Great Hall should be used. To implement this the splendid staircase, which swept up either side of the Great Hall to a balcony giving access to the principal bedrooms, had to be removed. This caused controversy locally for there were some who regarded the demolition of the staircase as an act of vandalism. There was even comment in the Daily Telegraph.

It was a grievous thing to see that elegant staircase taken down, but from a Claretian point of view it was unavoidable. Some of the stone slabs of the staircase were used to strengthen the path leading down to the beach. This path has been lost long since through cliff erosion but some of the Great Hall staircase can be discovered. The beautiful wrought iron balustrade was consigned to the basement. The Claretians constructed a choir balcony at the north end of the Chapel and some of the staircase balustrade was incorporated in it. This balcony collapsed with the general deterioration of the Great Hall in later years.

The Claretians made their College Chapel into a place of beauty according to the taste and devotional mood of the pre-Vatican II Church. The High Altar was adorned with rich baroque candlesticks and two ornate reliquaries and fronted with a fine antependium in the colour of the current church season or festival. Above the High Altar on the old balcony stood a life size statue of the Blessed Virgin Mary enthroned and supporting the Infant Jesus who pointed to her Immaculate Heart. The statue was presented by the Superior General of the Claretian Congregation, Father Peter Schweiger, and was executed by Claudio Rius of Barcelona.

Archbishop Cardinale leaving the Great Hall Chapel, 1965

On either side of the High Altar were heraldic shields in carved stone which a student carefully painted after due research into the correct heraldic colours. Above the High Altar were two windows containing medieval stained glass of the Blessed Virgin Mary and St. Andrew. Behind the Altar on its right hand side was a beautifully carved oak door showing St. Christopher carrying the Christ Child. The Chapel walls were freshly plastered and the stations of the Cross in carved wood bas-relief were mounted on them, seven on either side. All this has gone. Even the heraldic shields that might have survived have been hacked away by some wanton looter or vandal.

For those who knew and loved the chapel as a place of worship, its annihilation is a cause for sadness. But mercifully the magnificent stained glass window at its north end, named the Jesse window for its Tree of Jesse motive, was saved, preserved and re-installed in all its glory as part of the Castle Restoration. It is truly a wonderful sight to see.

The Jesse Window and students' choir loft.

CHRISTMAS IN THE COLLEGE

Just as Christmas and Easter had been happy celebrations for the Novices at the Castle, it was equally so for the students. Christmas, a time for cribs and decorations, here the students excelled. A miniature Bethlehem scene was created in the chapel, principally the work of an Austrian student who explained that in Austria the children are taught how to create Bethlehem scenes from natural materials for home, church and school.

Each Christmas that young Austrian produced a work of art. He went to the surrounding woods to collect moss, wood-bark, leaf mould and evergreen. He searched for stones and rockery of correct shape and size for his work. And as if this were not enough he created another Bethlehem scene above the fireplace in the conservatory, for this was the students' recreation area.

Garlands to decorate the chapel were made from holly and other evergreen leaves gathered in large quantities from the surrounding woods. Blanket needles and strong cord were used for threading each leaf one by one. It took hours for groups of students seated in the Octagonal Room and Ante-Library working patiently to make sufficient garlands to deck the Great Hall Chapel. These natural garlands were just right as decorations for the College Chapel in its dignified Great Hall setting. And what an unforgettable sight it was, the Chapel festooned with garlands and wreaths of evergreen, hand made by the students. From all that evergreen arose a sweet and delightful perfume. It was the scent of the forest and countryside.

If the Bethlehem scene and evergreen garlands brought an added beauty to the Chapel, what could be said of the Christmas tree? It did take up a fair amount of room, but everyone loves a Christmas tree. The students decorated the tree with silver tinsel painstakingly arranging each strand one by one with symmetrical precision on each branch. This slow and careful process took hours to complete but the final effect was worth all the effort. The Christmas tree looked as if it were covered with glistening icicles. The slightest movement in the air moved the tinsel ever so slightly creating a shimmering, sparkling effect with patterns of reflected light. It was truly remarkable to see.

And so the Midnight Mass of the Nativity was celebrated at Highcliffe Castle in traditional seasonal and festive surroundings. The student choir had practised assiduously, determined to make their polyphonic singing of the Mass just right while the Mass servers had rehearsed the ceremonies to perfection.

One year, to create additional atmosphere, a loudspeaker was fitted in the archway just outside the main entrance into the Great Hall Chapel. A recording of the bells from the Church of the Nativity in Bethlehem was played as visitors were arriving for Christmas Midnight Mass. It seemed quite effective at the time although there was a school of opinion that opposed recordings of church bells being used as a substitute for the real thing. But whatever the opinions were that Christmas, it did show imagination and resourcefulness on the part of the students.

On Christmas Day a priest could celebrate three different Masses of the Nativity either consecutively with no pause between them or separately at different hours and in different churches. Father Rector, who celebrated the Christmas Midnight Mass in the Great Hall Chapel, went on to celebrate his second and third Christmas Masses without pause. During the second Mass the student choir sang Christmas Carols for which many visitors stayed. As the third Mass began the students quietly said Morning Prayers and made a silent meditation on the great event at Bethlehem they were celebrating. They finished their meditation at the end of the third Mass.

Well, all this was a great deal of religion and since 'Twas the season to be Jolly' all the students betook themselves to the Conservatory where waiting to greet them was Santa himself in traditional red costume and cotton wool beard. During the two weeks leading up to Christmas all the students' mail had been held over and now Santa was here to distribute it to the rightful owners. It was a clever way of ensuring that all the students had plenty to open and unwrap on Christmas Day in the morning. There was hot tea with sandwiches, hot mince pies, cake and biscuits to restore those generous hearted young men who had worked so hard to help make the Chapel celebration of Christmas joyful and uplifting. For the rest of those early hours of Christmas morning some might doze in armchairs in the Conservatory or chat quietly round the log fire in the Library or take a breath of fresh air in the garden or spend a few more quiet moments in Chapel. No one bothered to turn into bed.

Breakfast was taken standing from a trolley brought up from the kitchen. The next task was to prepare the refectory for Christmas Lunch. The refectory tables, made by one of the students, were plain, bare and functional. But on Christmas Day they were covered with snowy white cloths, adorned with red candles and home-made decorations of pine cones and holly. There were Christmas crackers too and seasonally decorated paper napkins and gleaming wine glasses were to be seen.

The Community assembled for lunch in silence as usual, the Latin grace was said and there was a token reading that Father Rector ended with a tinkle of a little bell. He then raised the customary silence at meals with a suitable versicle and response. Immediately the waiters entered dressed as waiters should be, in black suits, gleaming white shirts, and black bow ties. They carried in the Christmas fare on great dishes from which everyone was able to help himself. Corks popped, wine was poured, crackers snapped and all tucked into traditional turkey and trimmings followed by customary Christmas pudding against seasonal background music played over the Tannoy system.

In the afternoon, after lunch, the students being young and vigorous worked off all that Christmas fare with a game of football. Those who were less sport minded enjoyed a long and refreshing walk along the beach. Then all reassembled for tea with Christmas cake and mince pies in abundance. After tea it was customary to have Solemn Benediction of the Blessed Sacrament in the Chapel and in the evening there was a film projected in the Library.

Another very pleasant feature of Christmas at Highcliffe was the students carol singing in Rothesay Drive. This was their way of saying "Happy Christmas" to the immediate neighbours of the College. Needless to say not a few doors opened to welcome in the choristers who were generously regaled and refreshed with Christmas spirits. It is certain that all those young students would have thought of home and parents and family at Christmas time and no doubt missed them not a little. But the Claretian Congregation always sought to foster a family spirit in all its Communities. Highcliffe was more than a college to its students, it was also their home. So all celebrations were family celebrations and there can be no doubt, everyone had a good time when they took place.

The Feast of St. Stephen or Boxing Day was a quieter occasion. For the students it was a free day to relax and perhaps rest a little. Board games were popular such as 'Monopoly', 'Cluedo', a horse race game called 'Totopoly', and one called 'Careers'. There was more football after lunch and television that was not seen in term time, was allowed in the evening, and was considered a great treat. The students certainly had a good Christmas and in later years might look back upon Christmas past at Highcliffe Castle with a certain nostalgia.

EASTER TIDE

Easter was the most important time in the year for the students at Highcliffe when they, with all Christians, commemorated the Passion and Death of our Lord upon the cross and his Glorious Resurrection. The spiritual preparation for the observance of Easter began on Ash Wednesday, starting the forty days season of Lent and recalling Jesus fasting in the desert for forty days and overcoming the temptations of the Devil, before beginning his public ministry.

On Ash Wednesday Christians go to church to receive the ashes that the priest blesses and with them makes a sign of the cross on their foreheads to remind them of their own mortality. For Christians the season of Lent is a time of prayer, self-denial and spiritual preparation for the commemoration of the Last Supper, Christ's death upon the Cross and his Rising from the Tomb. These core events of Christian belief are celebrated at the end of Lent during Holy Week that begins on Palm Sunday when the triumphal entry of Jesus into Jerusalem is recalled.

At Highcliffe the Palm Sunday celebration began at the South Garden Porch where the clergy, student choir and servers and visiting people gathered for the blessing of Palms which were given out to all those present. Then everyone went in solemn procession along the pathway, past the Drawing Room, and the Conservatory, along by the Library and the west side of the Great Hall and into the Chapel. This represented Jesus entering Jerusalem in triumph. Inside the Chapel the priest and two deacons sang the Gospel story of the Arrest, Trial and Crucifixion of Jesus as it is written in Matthew's Gospel.

On Maundy Thursday, Thursday of Holy Week, the evening Mass of the Lord's Supper was celebrated in the College Chapel. This commemorated Jesus and his twelve Apostles eating the

Last Supper together in the upper room and Jesus instituting the Eucharist and Holy Communion and founding the Priesthood. The Evening Mass also recalled how Jesus washed the Apostles' feet and this was re-enacted by the priest ritually bathing the feet of twelve people.

After the Mass the reserved Sacrament was carried in procession to an altar of repose prepared for its reception in the Octagonal Room. It was customary for students and visitors to keep vigil at this altar until midnight. Meanwhile all altar cloths, candles, and other adornments were removed from the Chapel. The tabernacle on the altar was left empty, unveiled and with its door fully open.

Good Friday was a day of great mourning when Jesus encountered death on the Cross suffering for the Redemption of all people. The solemn liturgy of Good Friday Commemorated the Redemption of the world. The priest and two deacons sang the Gospel account of the Arrest, Trial and Crucifixion of Jesus as written by John. After this the crucifix was carried into the Chapel in procession and placed in front of the altar. Then the priest, servers, choir and people all came up one by one to kiss the feet of the crucifix. This was called 'the Veneration of the Cross'. Finally the reserved Sacrament was brought from the Altar of Repose of Maundy Thursday and everyone received Holy Communion.

Saturday was called Holy Saturday when the Easter Vigil took place, followed by the Mass of Easter Night. Everyone assembled outside the Chapel entrance at dusk overlooked by the towering height of the North Portico. There the priest blessed the first Fire of Easter from which he lit the Paschal Candle that symbolised the risen Christ. The Deacon then carried the Paschal Candle in solemn procession followed by the priest, servers, choir and people, all carrying unlit candles. The procession stopped three times, at the entrance of the chapel, at the middle of the nave and finally in the sanctuary. At each stop the Deacon proclaimed the Light of Christ. After the first proclamation the officiating priest lit his candle, from the Paschal Candle, after the second, the servers' and choir's candles were lit and after the final proclamation all the people's candles were lit and the lights in the darkened Chapel were all switched on. This Blessing of the New Fire and the Paschal Candle and the solemn procession of entry added up to an impressive ceremony in the atmospheric surroundings of the dusk enshrouded Great Portico towering into the darkness and the lofty Great Hall.

The Chapel, its darkness broken by the solitary flame of the Paschal Candle, then by the tapers of the priest, choir and servers was then suddenly flooded with light at the final proclamation. It was a wonderful setting for these ancient and hallowed rituals.

The proclamation of the Easter Message sung by the Deacon then followed. Known as the 'Exsultet' it expounded the beautiful symbolic meaning of the Paschal Candle. Sung in Latin plainsong the Exsultet had a haunting beauty all of its own heightened no doubt by the atmosphere of Easter night when people of deep religious convictions gather to rejoice over Christ risen from the tomb.

Then the Lessons were read and the first part of the Litany of the Saints was sung. As the Chapel was not a Parish Church the Blessing of Baptismal Water was omitted but everyone made a public solemn renewal of their Baptismal Vows and the second part of the Litany was sung. It was then time for the Mass of Easter Night. It was full of the joy of the Resurrection and when the celebrant intoned the Gloria in Excelsis Deo the Chapel organ burst forth in a splendid voluntary and the bells, silent since Maundy Thursday, rang out.

All these Holy Week services were in Latin and according to the old Tridentine liturgy. The choir sang to a very high standard and the serving at the altar was impeccable.

Highcliffe Castle, North Portico.

45

It was probably only in a seminary or a monastery or cathedral that full justice could be done to a complicated liturgy all in Latin and difficult music. When the liturgy was carried out in the full manner it could be a moving experience. Holy Week at Highcliffe Castle was something to be remembered. And Lady Waterford, to whom religion was a matter of the greatest importance, would she have rejoiced to have seen these ancient and holy rites performed in her own stately home? One feels it might well have given her the greatest satisfaction.

FURTHER FESTIVALS

The Feast day of the Claretian Founder, St. Anthony Claret on 23rd October was a holiday for the students. It was celebrated with High Mass in the College Chapel in the morning and later there was an excellent lunch when, naturally, claret wine was served. Some members of the Faculty were persuaded to join in the afternoon friendly football match and there were some skilled players among them. In the evening a film was shown in the Library. But curiously, St. Anthony Claret's day seemed upstaged by the celebrations on Father Rector's birthday, called his Feast day. For this, many guests arrived from the other Claretian houses and all the local clergy were invited too. Father Rector celebrated High Mass and the student choir was always in excellent voice. The celebratory birthday lunch was almost on the scale and magnificence of Christmas Day.

In the afternoon the students gave an entertainment in the Library, usually a drama production with musical interludes played by student solo instrumentalists. From the giving of these entertainments sprang an increasing interest in drama and the students went on to produce a number of full length plays which were acted before wider audiences.

MUSIC AND DRAMA

There was a very good standard of music in the College and the student choir gained a local reputation for the high quality of its singing at religious services and it occasionally sang in local Catholic churches. There were also instrumentalists and some students received piano, violin and flute lessons. One Austrian student attended advanced flute lessons given by Norman McLelland, the celebrated flautist then with the Bournemouth Symphony Orchestra. This valuable contact led to visits to Highcliffe Castle by members of the Bournemouth Symphony Orchestra to give private music recitals to the students and faculty. These took place in the Drawing Room, a wonderful setting for these musical evenings that were a deeply appreciated feature of college life.

The Bournemouth Symphony Orchestra under its then conductor Charles Groves, this was before his accolade, also came to provide the music for a performance of scenes from Shakespeare given by the Bournemouth Shakespeare Company. This memorable performance took place on a summer's evening on the grassed area immediately overlooking the Castle south front and lawns. At that time a wide gated entrance opened from the lawns onto this stretch of grass that extended to the cliff edge. Also in those says there were extensive rhododendron bushes either side of the grassed section and these provided natural wings for the artistes. It was a beautiful setting for an outdoor production of Shakespeare. Seating for the large audience was arranged on the lawns.

Among plays which the students produced were the morality play, *Everyman*; T.S. Eliot's *Murder in the Cathedral*, the story of the martyrdom of St. Thomas à Becket in Canterbury Cathedral; *Challenge*, a play about St. Edmund Campion in Elizabethan times by Margaret Hotine and *Morning Departure*, Kenneth Woolard's drama concerning the failed attempt to rescue the crew of a sunken Royal Navy submarine. The Royal Navy submarine base at Portland loaned submarine escape gear and uniforms for *Morning Departure*. A gifted German student created a very realistic stage set of the inside of the sunken submarine at the south end of the Library. Visiting Royal Naval officers Lt. Crickmore R.N. of H.M.S. Osprey, Commander Garson, R.N. of H.M.S. Chaser and Lt. Forbes, R.N commanding the submarine Sea Scout from Portland were impressed by its realism and accuracy *Morning Departure* was first acted in the Library at Highcliffe and then at the Catholic senior school in Hayes. The stage set was dismantled and re-assembled on the school stage.

When the students came to produce *Murder in the Cathedral* they turned to the Bournemouth Shakespeare Company for help that was generously given. Costumes and sword were loaned but the Archbishop's robes came courtesy of Oscott College. *Murder in the Cathedral* was produced first in the library at Highcliffe. The arch between the ante-library and library was the setting for the play. A further production took place in the College Chapel and there were two more productions in the parish church at Hayes.

Then in January 1965 came the last students' production to take place in Highcliffe Castle. This was Gilbert and Sullivan's *H.M.S. Pinafore*, which was presented on two nights to a large and appreciative audience. The students were very amused when a lady in the audience commented that she did not think the students would have been allowed to recruit girls from the village to sing in the cast. Wigs and skilful make-up had clearly done the trick.

Highcliffe Castle West Wing

49

FRIENDS AND HELPERS

Rothesay Drive was constructed and its pleasant bungalows built after the Claretians came to Highcliffe. They were the first close neighbours and many of them became kind and generous friends to the College. There were other good friends living in and around Highcliffe and as this army of friends grew and their desire to help the College increased so the Claretian Guild was formed. There were so many good and kind Guild members who helped the College with immense generosity in countless different ways. But there was perhaps one who will always be remembered with affection and gratitude by Claretians and Guild members who were associated with Highcliffe Castle. This was Nurse Ellwood, the local District Nurse, who lived in Rothesay Drive within clear view of the Castle. She was one of the founder members of the Guild and a constant friend and helper right up to the day the Claretians left. She is surely remembered with great esteem by all who were at Highcliffe Castle for one period or another of the Claretian era.

CHRISTMAS AND SUMMER FETES

It was the Claretian Guild which promoted and organised those two hugely popular events of the College year, the Christmas Bazaar and the Summer Fete.

The Christmas Bazaar occupied the State Rooms, the Drawing Room, the Library, the Octagonal Room and the Dining Room. The visitors arrived in crowds and entered by the garden porch. Everyone had a good time and of course Santa arrived with gifts for the children.

But if the Christmas Bazaar was a popular event then the annual

Summer Fete at Highcliffe Castle was a date in everyone's diary. Local people flocked in, delighted to have the opportunity of seeing inside the Castle and wandering through its grounds. The surrounding Catholic parishes gave their support and coaches arrived from the Claretian parish at Hayes bringing parishioners to join in the fun and to help. It was customary to invite a celebrity to open the fete. One year it was the local Member of Parliament and another year it was Ted Kavanagh famous in his day as a radio comedy scriptwriter and for his association with Tommy Handley, top radio comedian of his day, whom those born before 1940 should remember.

Among those who came to open a summer fete at the Castle the most interesting must have been Sir Shane Leslie who represented three generations from the Castle's past history. His grandmother, Lady Constance Leslie had been a close friend of Lady Waterford and his father, Sir John Leslie, the second Baronet, was one of the group who commissioned the celebrated statue of Lady Waterford as a sign of their love and esteem for her and which now stands in the ante-library. Sir Shane spent holidays at the Castle as a boy and was a frequent visitor when Major General Stuart-Wortley was the Castle's owner and with whom he became a close friend. Sir Shane delivered a fascinating talk about the old days at Highcliffe and the famous people who visited it, many of whom he knew well. Sir Shane stood in the garden porch to give his address and open the fete, a striking figure, tall and distinguished, his voice as clear as a bell. This talk was recorded but it is doubtful that the tape still exists.

Sir Shane had visited the Castle earlier that year and met Father Crook who asked his visitor to autograph one of his books in the library. This contact led to Sir Shane being invited to open the next Summer Fete at Highcliffe Castle, which he gladly did.

At the first of the summer fetes the visitors were all enjoying themselves so much that no one wanted to go home. How could they all be politely advised that the fete was now drawing to a close and it was time to leave, wondered the organisers. Now there had been recorded music all afternoon playing over the Tannoy system. "Did the music department have the National Anthem among its records?" asked a student because if they did, playing it would clearly convey that it was home time. Indeed there was a record of the National Anthem that was at once played. There was immediate silence as the men stood to attention and the ladies ceased conversing. One German student with keen monarchist sympathies was particularly impressed. "Such discipline", he declared. It had worked. Once the National Anthem ended, everyone began to leave. After that the playing of the National Anthem customarily closed the summer fete at Highcliffe Castle but a question suggests itself - would it do so today?

STUDENTS AT PLAY

Of course the students didn't spend all their time studying and praying. They had free time and holidays as well and made the most of them.

There was a good measure of sport and the students had a reasonable football team that played nearby R.A.F and Army sides and local Catholic schools. They also had a regular fixture against the Salesian students who were studying for the priesthood in their college at Melchet Court, which closed down many years ago. The Salesians are a modern Congregation whose principal work was teaching in their own Salesian colleges which all had an enviable reputation for academic excellence.

One memorable match was on an Ash Wednesday afternoon

when eleven fasting students lost rather heavily to an R.A.F. side. After this Ash Wednesday game the students were taken to the dining hall where huge helpings of sausages, bacon, black pudding, eggs, beans tomatoes and chips were placed before them. Now Ash Wednesday is the first day of the penitential season of Lent and it was a strict church day of fasting and abstinence when Catholics take only a restricted amount of food and eat no meat at all. A normal lunch was allowed but only the merest taste at breakfast and supper and no afternoon tea with bread and jam. Naturally the Congregation and its students took this very seriously indeed and strictly observed the Church Laws of Fast and Abstinence.

So how did they face this moral dilemma caused by generous R.A.F. hospitality of sausages, bacon, black pudding and trimmings served by the ton? Perhaps the solution may have lain in the strict doctrine once taught to all Catholic children that it was a very serious sin to waste food. Good sense would have surely prevailed to everyone's satisfaction on that far off Ash Wednesday afternoon. Per Ardua ad Astra!

Cricket was tried with very little success but the students laid out a tennis court with an all weather concrete surface at the side of the west lawn. Sheltered seating was constructed from sheet metal panels taken from the disused children's home toilets situated in the east end of the Conservatory. The tennis court was also used for four a side football. Unfortunately using the tennis court for football rendered its concrete surface very slippery but happily there were no serious tumbles or injuries. The tennis and football tournaments played on that home-made court were very popular. There is no trace of it today.

A generous benefactor presented the students with a full size slate snooker table with all accessories. Two experts from the company that supplied the table set it up in the Conservatory. Snooker became a favourite pastime and tournaments caused great interest and excitement. There were some very skilled players among the students. Table tennis in the Conservatory was also widely enjoyed and again there were many skilful players and keenly contested tournaments.

Although all cinemas were strictly out of bounds, there were occasional visits to see films considered to be suitable for the students. Suitability consisted in being of a religious content. Among some of the films seen in the local cinemas were Cecil B. De Mille's *The Ten Commandments* featuring Charlton Heston, *Inherit the Wind* with Spencer Tracy and *The Nun's Story* with Audrey Hepburn.

On the day before the new academic year began in October there was a day's outing, sometimes by hired coach. Occasionally in holiday time there was a 'day out' when all the students dispersed with meagre rations and a small allowance to roam the countryside or the shoreline. Some students were discovered to have hitchhiked as far as London. Very enterprising but officially disapproved of. A collection of bicycles was amassed largely from relatives of students and benefactors. One was a folding bicycle as issued to parachutists during the war. The bicycles were kept in the old wine bins in the charge of one of the students who made an excellent job of keeping them all in good running order. It was quite popular to go for a spin on a Sunday afternoon, usually towards the New Forest.

But the most spectacular spin of all took place in the summer of 1964 when seven students cycled 350 miles to Danby Hall, the White Fathers Missionary College near Leyburn in Yorkshire where they spent eleven days holiday.

Aerial Photograph of Highcliffe Castle, c. 1955

55

THE LONG SUMMER VACATION

The college year ended in early July with written examinations. After this there were no more lectures until October. It was a long time to fill as the students did not go home during this 'vacation' time. So what was to become of them during all those weeks from July to October; how would they fill all that time? There were various solutions.

One year, for instance, all the students were transported to Buckden Towers to work at painting and decorating and general D.I.Y. at the newly acquired school buildings. They must have had a lot of fun during this welcome change from academic life.

But there was one great enterprise which went to occupy the weeks of summer for some years. The Claretians needed to find the money necessary to finance its three training centres at Highcliffe, Backwell Hill and Buckden. Now an enterprising American priest had established a form of football pool in Hayes to raise funds for running the parish. The resourceful priest suggested that a similar football pool be set up to bring in money to help with the expenses of training postulants, novices and students. He recommended that the students should go home in the summer to promote the new Claretian football pool. They would do this by finding agents to enrol regular weekly subscribers to the pool. This was done in the nineteen fifties and the students dispersed to increase the pools earning capacity in their own parishes. The scheme prospered and it was found necessary to appoint a priest to travel around visiting the agents of the football pool to encourage and help them. The priest had himself been a student at Highcliffe and this helped him to give a clear picture of what the agents were helping through their work. And so he travelled to Lancashire, Yorkshire, Cumberland on into Scotland and across the sea to Ireland. The football pool was given the dignified name of 'The Claretian Seminaries

Association' and it became a significant source of revenue towards the cost of training students for the priesthood.

Another Claretian enterprise during the summer at Highcliffe was the running of 'Retreat Holidays' for boys. Their purpose was to give boys the opportunity to live for one week in a Religious House and to be able to ask questions about the priesthood and the religious life.

They were run by the priest who had responsibility for those seeking to join the Claretian Congregation. He was known as the 'Director of Vocations'.

These Retreat Holidays were very well subscribed and about sixty boys who came from all over England were accepted for each week. They were also very well run. The mornings were the retreat part with lively and interesting talks followed by even more lively question and answer sessions. Boys chiefly wanted to know how long it took to become a priest and what would they have to study. They also had workshops that were very informative and productive.

The afternoon was free time spent mostly on the beach and a fine rapport was struck up between the Vocations Director with his student assistants and those lively young 'retreatants'. There was no pressure applied to these boys, no manipulation, no attempts at persuasion. All that was given was matter of fact information and impartial advice. Nevertheless many of these boys subsequently applied to join the Claretian Junior Seminary at Buckden.

It has been said that the thoughts of youth are long deep thoughts and serious mindedness and earnestness of some of the boys need not be doubted. One of them wrote an article 'Thoughts on a Claretian Retreat Holiday' published in the *Claretian*, September-October 1964. Here was a young neophyte indeed and one cannot but be moved by the depth and idealism of the thoughts he expressed.

Whether a teenager would or could write in this manner today is open to question as is the likelihood of a retreat holiday attracting as many boys with the same idealism and enthusiasm as those of 1964.

SUNSET AT HIGHCLIFFE

In the *Claretian Chronicle*, a well presented and immensely readable little news magazine produced by the students at Highcliffe, the editor observed in the December issue of 1959 that until 1950 there were only two small Claretian communities in England at Hayes and Loughton. "Now after ten short years there is Highcliffe Castle, with a community of 30 Claretians. There are six studying in Rome. At Backwell House there are 17 Novices. At Buckden there are 50 enthusiastic Postulants ages 11 to 16 receiving their education before entering the Novitiate. It is a wonderful growth indeed. And the one man chiefly responsible is our dear Provincial, Father Stephen Emaldia."

On reflection, what an extraordinary act of faith it had been to purchase Highcliffe Castle in 1953. If it were to be a college, where were the students to fill it? There were just one English and one Irish plus a co-opted German student who had made their Noviciate in Spain. In the event it became the Noviciate with Father Crook and his three Novices who on their first day boiled water for tea on an open fire on the Sundial Walk at the foot of the Conservatory steps.

But the Editor's words in the December 1959 edition of the *Claretian Chronicle* showed that all was very well indeed and that Father Emaldia's act of faith was truly justified. All the Claretians had every ground for viewing the future with optimism as they went from strength to strength.

The *Claretian Chronicle* and its successor *The Claretian*, both reflected the optimism, enthusiasm and self-confidence that was felt among the Claretians at that time, particularly the students. To read these well produced magazines today with their news and reports from all the centres of Claretian training at Buckden, Backwell and Highcliffe is to capture once again the spirit of youthful idealism and commitment that prevailed at that time. Perhaps the tone could best be described as exuberant but there was substance too because then, those young men had high ideals, deep faith and a true sense of being called to serve God and His Church. They reflected an age of faith and religious practice that has faded into the past. There is still faith and religious practice to be found today, but where have all the young men gone?

Boy and dolphin fountain by the South Portico

59

But with the dawn of the 1960's a year later, a decline set in. Students began leaving Highcliffe in considerable numbers, applicants for the Novitiate at Backwell dwindled and there was a fall in the number of pupils at Buckden. By 1966 the student body was so badly diminished that it became necessary to rationalise the situation. This was done by enrolling a cadre of students at Heythrop College and finding a new House of Studies at Radford near Oxford for them to live in. The Claretians now had no use for Highcliffe Castle whose acquisition thirteen years earlier had caused such excitement, so they sold it apparently to some businessmen although to this day the transaction remains obscure.

The Claretians left behind substantial goods and chattels including a large quantity of books in the Library. Some of these books bearing the 'Ex Libris Claretian Missionaries Highcliffe Castle' label mysteriously found their way into sundry bookshops including Foyles in London. Eyewitnesses describe a Marie Celeste impression as if the Claretians had simply got up and gone out of the Castle for a walk and not returned.

The disintegration of the fabric of Highcliffe Castle and the mysterious fires (after the Claretians left) are a sad story. So much of what was in place when the Claretians arrived in 1953 has gone and the casualty list is a long one due to deterioration, vandalism, pillage and fire. Gone from the Conservatory are the Kaisers windows, the Jumièges gargoyles and the bronze statue of Major General Stuart Wortley's daughter, Bettine, as a child costumed for a fancy dress party as Joan of Arc. The imitation bookcase doors no longer deceive the eye in the Library. The de Rothesay achievements atop the doors in the Octagonal Room are scorched and scarred beyond recognition, the de la Fontaine bas-relief panels are gone. The Drawing Room is now a shell, its ornate gilded ceiling gone. St. Ouen has disappeared from the garden porch, the fishpond has been filled in, and the boy on the dolphin has been sold to a film star. Even the sundial, a relic of the first Highcliffe has been taken away. From the Great Hall everything is gone. The Dining Room has lost its fireplace and stained glass and the massive portrait of King George IV hangs there no longer.

But there are some notable survivors and visitors can still enjoy the Jesse window, gloriously restored in the Great Hall. Lady Waterford is back and has resumed her place in the ante-library. The Conservatory, Library and Octagonal Room are airy, elegant and welcoming with beautifully laid out exhibitions to be seen and fascinating relics of Highcliffe's past on display.

The Great Hall before its conversion into the College Chapel

61

THE STUDENTS THAT WERE

Pause to reflect on the students who came to Highcliffe in the early 1950's. All were born before 1940 and World War II had overshadowed their childhood and adolescence. As students they lived in a different world. Winston Churchill was Prime Minister, young men were being called up into the Armed Forces at eighteen, the voting age was twenty-one, food was still rationed. There was an 11+ examination. Most children left school at fifteen, some at sixteen and a tiny minority made university. There was corporal punishment in schools and capital punishment for murderers who were hanged. Parents, teachers, employers and policemen were respected and obeyed. No one was afraid to be out after dark. Children could visit London parks, museums and exhibitions unaccompanied with no fears for their safety. There was only four hours black and white television each day shown on a single (B.B.C.) channel on twelve-inch screens.

The Catholic Church was strong, confident, self-assured. Converts flocked into its fold; the seminaries were full, Religious Orders and Congregations for men and women flourished. The second Vatican Council was yet to be.

Against this background the students at Highcliffe led a strict life of prayer and study and had plenty of manual work. They didn't go to discos, nightclubs, cinemas, football matches, pubs, cafes or restaurants. They didn't see newspapers or magazines and watched television only at Christmas. They couldn't come and go as they pleased, permission and an important reason were required before going out. They did not go home for holidays. And all of them, when they came to Highcliffe, had a burning desire to become a Catholic priest - it was all that mattered. And they all faithfully observed a catalogue of very strict rules.

It is apparent that the Claretian Congregation and for that matter the Church itself is unable to attract and inspire large numbers of young men to live such a life today. That those past students at Highcliffe did is noteworthy and food for thought.

They possessed a diversity of talents and they were an energetic, creative and constructive group of young men. Apart from a high proportion of excellent footballers (all those Germans), adroit tennis players and skilled exponents of snooker and table tennis there were electricians, carpenters, writers, singers, actors and organisers. They could re-wire a building and install fuse boxes, build walls, lay a road, construct a tennis court, make furniture, play musical instruments, sing Latin motets or comic opera, act high drama, write articles, produce magazines, keep bees, plumb in a bathroom - the list goes on and on. They looked after Highcliffe Castle and its grounds, cleaning, repairing, renewing, gardening - they appreciated the beauty of their surroundings and many loved the place.

By the end of the 1960's Highcliffe Castle and Backwell Hill House had been sold, there being no longer any students or novices to fill them. Buckden had ceased to be a junior seminary for the same reason. The edifice that had risen so impressively from 1953 to 1966 had crumbled and fallen before the very eyes of its builders. But no one in the confident and self-assured 1950's could have foreseen the calamitous falling off in religious observances and the sharp decrease in vocations to the priesthood which was to descend like a blight on the Catholic Church during the next decade and still obtains today. In 1951 an article in the *Clergy Review* remarked that it was thought that the demand for priests would soon outstrip the capacity of the five existing seminaries in England and the five colleges in Rome, Spain and Portugal.

In 1999 those seminaries and colleges still open, four in England, three abroad, have 250 students between them. One of them, that had 384 alumni and 36 teachers in 1951, has less than 40 students today.

In 1999 the number of priests ordained for sixteen dioceses in England and Wales was 50. Six other dioceses had no priests ordained at all. In the same year nineteen priests were ordained from Religious Orders and Congregations of which there are 56 in England and Wales.

The malaise is everywhere.

The Catholic directory reveals that the Claretians are currently administering six parishes in England and Wales, including the foundation parish at Hayes and Buckden its former junior seminary.

There are just thirteen Claretian Fathers for the task, a number of whom are of retirement age, and there is no college, noviciate or junior seminary to meet the needs of the future.

ECUMENISM AT THE COLLEGE

The ecumenical movement began in the Roman Catholic Church during the 1960's towards the end of the Claretian era at Highcliffe Castle. It was one of the many developments arising from the second Vatican Council (1962-1965) and Roman Catholic attitudes towards the other Christian denominations took a marked change for the better. Old hostilities and antipathies that had been contrary to the Christian spirit began to dissolve and disappear.

The Vicar of Highcliffe, the Reverend R.T. Barnett had been a friend to the Claretians from the very start. He used to pull Father Crook's leg by quoting from the old version of the popular hymn

All Things Bright and Beautiful the now disused verse which ran, "The rich man in his castle, the poor man at his gate", in reference to themselves. Father Crook certainly lived in a castle and the Vicarage stood near its gate.

A tremendous rapport existed between these two priests, which in 1953 was far in advance of the ecumenical age yet to be born. The Reverend R.T. Barnett took a great interest in Highcliffe Castle and when a history and guide was proposed he helped its author with valuable archive material.

By the mid sixties ecumenism was on everybody's agenda and the Claretian College became involved in Church Unity Services with its then rector being invited to preach. One took place at St. Marks Church in 1965 and several students were ushered into the traditionally known Highcliffe Castle pew reserved for the occupants of the Castle.

The Vicar expressed his joy at seeing occupants from Highcliffe Castle seated in this pew for the first time in many years. It was a historic occasion from every point of view and the Editor of the Bournemouth Echo made it front page news.

SUNRISE

Highcliffe Castle has entered a new epoch. For over a century the titled, the wealthy and the privileged held sway here. They are all gone now. The childrens' home came and went in a blink of an eye. Then the Claretians arrived and flourished. When Father Crook asked me to write a history and guide of Highcliffe Castle in 1960 it was my belief that the Claretians would continue to prosper indefinitely. Highcliffe Castle would always be a Claretian place.

Profession of Novices at Backwell Hill House, August 1959
Fr. Emaldia on left of photograph, bespectacle. Fr. Crook on right

But they faded away and the Castle faded too. Now it has come back to life, and it is a joy to see the day. What is more, Highcliffe Castle at the turn of the century and beyond is for everyone to enjoy. It is not exclusive to grandees or high-principled religious, it belongs to you and to me, it is for all of us, it extends its friendly welcome to everyone.

Highcliffe Castle exercises a certain spell over the hearts and minds of all who come to know it. How else can be explained its marvellous resurrection and the army of eager volunteers who tirelessly advance its interests and support its needs?

Highcliffe Castle will go on capturing hearts and loyalties. Visitors will continue to wonder at the beauty of the place and to catch the pervading atmosphere of welcome and friendliness that seems to linger like a palpable presence in its rooms and grounds. On and on it will go. Floreat Highcliffe Castle. Its place in the 21st century is assured.

ENVOI

Father Stephen Emaldia, C.M.F. launched the Claretian dream in England when he made the courageous decision to purchase Highcliffe Castle. We need not doubt that Father Arthur Crook, C.M.F. urged, encouraged even persuaded him to do so. Their names are part of the Castle's history now. Loved and respected by all their colleagues and all who knew them, Father Emaldia and Father Crook brought the Claretians to Highcliffe Castle. When the Castle was finally sold in 1967 both these venerable Fathers had retired from high office in the Claretian Provincial government. It was others who decided to sell Highcliffe Castle having judged it as being of no use to the Congregation. How Father Emaldia and Father Crook would rejoice to see Highcliffe so magnificently restored, for both regarded it as 'the jewel in the crown' of Claretian endeavour and achievement in England.

Father Crook would no doubt have described the Highcliffe Castle of today as 'Paradise Regained'.

The students were the last people to actually live in the Castle and to look upon it as their home. They were its last residents. They brought life and enthusiastic activity to Highcliffe Castle and played a distinctive part in its history and they surely recall it with affection wherever they are today. Let those young men of 1953-66 be remembered, for as Highcliffe Castle waxes in its rebirth and renewal, it too is young again.